MW01491723

The Jezebel Spirit

DAVE WILLIAMS

The Jezebel Spirit

*Freeing Yourself from
the Spirit of Control*

DAVE WILLIAMS

The Jezebel Spirit
Freeing Yourself from the Spirit of Control

Unless otherwise noted, Scripture quotations are taken from the King James Version of the Bible.

Scripture quotations noted TLB are from *The Living Bible*, Copyright © 1971. Used by permission of Tyndale House Publishers, Inc., Wheaton, Illinois 60189. All rights reserved.

Scripture quotations noted NIV are from the *Holy Bible, New International Version* ®. Copyright © 1973, 1978, 1984 by International Bible Society. Used by permission of Zondervan Publishing House. All rights reserved.

Published by

DECAPOLIS
PUBLISHING

Printed in the United States of America

BOOKS BY DAVE WILLIAMS

Contents

There is a powerful,
spiritual principality that
can seduce your life.

Chapter 1

The Jezebel Spirit

Have you ever experienced the feeling of being manipulated or controlled by another human being?

It happened to me when a fellow ran a red light, hit the right side of my car, and broke my shoulder. I had to deal with a particular insurance company that advertises "fast and friendly service." They weren't fast, and they weren't friendly, at least not to me. In fact, they were just the opposite, slow and unfriendly. I felt as though I was being manipulated and controlled. I felt out of control.

Out Of Control

When you feel out of control, it's a dangerous place to be. Why? Because there is a powerful, spiritual principality that can seduce your life at that point and attach itself to you. I think I was probably falling into that trap at the time. It was the most uncomfortable, out-of-control-type of feeling that I have ever experienced. I felt that even though the insurance company did everything *legally*, right to the outer edge of the law, they did *nothing* ethically or morally. It was a terrible feeling being knocked around by these disorganized, ineffectual people — forced to go here, forced to fill out this, forced to do this, and forced to do that. It was almost like some sort of bondage. After a year of dealing with this "Jezebel" insurance company, I had accumulated two huge boxes of paperwork, forms, receipts, duplicates, and triplicates. I had to use a wheeled-cart to take all the paperwork to storage.

There are people who, every day of their lives, feel controlled by other people. It may be a wife who tries to control her husband. There are some wives that want so badly to see their husbands saved that they actually resort to manipulation. This almost always has the opposite effect and ends up keeping their husbands away from God's kingdom.

There are husbands that, rather than motivating by love, try to motivate by intimidation, guilt, and manipulation.

I'm going to teach you about a spiritual principality that seeks to seduce, dominate, control, manipulate, and intimidate your life — the Jezebel spirit — and I want to show you how to break it off your life.

Now I want you to know something. One of my goals as a pastor is to have the best protected flock in the world. Whenever I make a decision, it is always with the flock's best interest at heart. I am protecting my flock from something, even when they don't realize it.

When a godly pastor makes a decision that you don't understand, you can do one of two things. You can say, "I don't want to be under that pastor's protection." You can leave the church if you want. Or you can say, "That man is my pastor; I trust him, and I thank God I have a pastor who wants to protect me." As a pastor, I'm trying to protect you right now from the Jezebel spirit by writing this book.

Every young pastor ought to read what I'm about to share with you. Because the fact is, for every forty pastors, only three survive. Thirty-seven out of every forty pastors eventually leave the ministry altogether. During times of great discouragement and times of warfare-like oppression, only three out of forty pastors survive. That's why I wish every young pastor could read what I'm going to share with you in this little book. It might help them through the rough sailing and the "bumps in the road."

The "Greater Works" Generation

I believe we are the "Greater Works Generation." Jesus said:

> Verily, verily, I say unto you, He that believeth on me, the works that I do shall he do also; and

> greater *works* than these shall he do; because I
> go unto my Father.
>
> —John 14:12

We are that "Greater Works Generation," the generation that believes the revelation of Jesus' supernatural promises, and the devil knows it.

Every time a fresh wave of God's Spirit approaches, Satan enlists and mobilizes opposition. It's as if he senses something big is coming and works feverishly to thwart it at the onset. He senses God's anointing waxing great, even though the devil has no prophetic insight whatsoever. If you don't believe that Satan has absolutely no clear insight into the future, just listen to people who've talked to the psychics.

"Call 1-900-dial-a-demon." Here's a typical conversation with a so-called psychic:

PSYCHIC: "Honey, I'm sensing there's somebody in your family… "J", I'm getting the letter "J"."

CALLER: "Is it, ah, is it … Jerry?"

PSYCHIC: "Oh, yes, Honey, that's what I was thinking. Um, I'm seeing a dog. Do you have a dog, Sweetheart?"

CALLER: "Well, my Aunt Betsy has a dog."

PSYCHIC: "Ah, ha. I was picking up vibes concerning a Betsy. Yes, that's exactly what was coming to me."

It doesn't take too much sense to see what's going on with these so-called psychics. The point is, the devil has no real, clear insight into the future. He can't even read your mind. He can just play games with you.

In all seriousness, whenever a miracle wave of the Holy Spirit is about to be launched, where the dead are raised to life and thousands are swept into the Kingdom of God, the devil reads the indicators and launches a counter-attack with Jezebelian spirits that resist repentance, hate humility, and work intensely to hinder or halt the approaching revival.

One year I knew, by the Spirit of God, that there was something in our church in Lansing that was hindering the greater works Jesus foretold. I gathered together some of our leaders and defined what I was sensing. I was sensing a spirit of competitiveness and an attitude of complacency in our church. This was preventing us from reaching our greatest heights in God.

At our meeting, a couple of people repented of the spirit of competitiveness, and some repented of complacency — the "I'm just here for a paycheck, and that's all" attitude.

Something Was Hindering

But there was something else. There seemed to be something more, some blockage, eluding us. I knew something bigger was hindering the great vision God had placed upon our church; only I couldn't identify it. Whatever it was, it didn't have the identifying factors that the principality Leviathan has, whom we've faced before and whom we've dealt with. It didn't have the same identifying features of Belial, the powerful dark principality that seeks to make people's lives and work seem worthless. What was it?

During that time, one of my personal prayer partners gave me a video of a man talking about a particular spirit that was on the loose against the Church, particularly in America. I thought it was interesting. Then CBN did a special segment with a man who talked about this same spirit that has been loosed on America. About that same time, I felt impressed to talk with my staff in a staff letter about the spirit of Jezebel as I saw it. I had begun to identify the spirit that was hindering our church as "the spirit of Jezebel."

After I published that staff letter and shared some of the characteristics of the spirit of Jezebel, which I'm going to give you, I found a small book by Francis Frangipane sitting on my desk. It was simply called, *The Jezebel Spirit,* and there was a note on it asking me for the approval to sell it in our book store. I sat down and read it in less than an hour. I wrote down little notes and realized that I was right; our church *was* being attacked by the Jezebel spirit.

I'm not saying any one person in particular necessarily carried the Jezebel spirit, but I knew that somewhere there was a Jezebel spirit trying to hinder the work of the Holy Spirit.

An Evangelist Finds Jezebel

I later turned on a tape somebody gave me, and it was an evangelist saying that he had a dream. He was on a platform, and there wasn't a whole lot happening. He noticed a woman standing on the platform with him, and he didn't like her being there. He wondered why none of his staff was removing her. It was like they didn't see her. Finally, he got up and rebuked her in the name of Jesus, and she disappeared — just vanished into thin air. At this time, he did not know who that woman was.

However, after that spirit vanished, the supernatural floodgates of the Holy Spirit opened up. The evangelist came down into the audience where there were three sections of people. He came to the first section of people and said, "We're going to worship God," and he started singing "How Great Thou Art." And when he got to the line "I in awesome wonder," everybody in that section fell to the floor under the power of God.

He then walked over to the second section and said, "Folks, we're going to sing 'How Great Thou Art,'" and when they got to the part "I in awesome wonder," they all fell under the power of the Holy Spirit. Just then rain started coming out of Heaven and drenched them all.

Finally, he came to the third section and said, "Sing it with me," and when they got to the part "I in awesome wonder," they all fell under the power of the Holy Spirit, and fire started coming down from Heaven.

One day, he was telling his wife about the strange dream. She looked surprised and excitedly told him, "Honey, I had that same dream five weeks ago." She told him, "I've got a book by Francis Frangipane you need to read."

So the evangelist sat down to read this little book about the Jezebel spirit. He then realized exactly who that woman on the platform in his dream was. His ministry had come under the influence of the Jezebel spirit, and it had to be dealt with.

He offered the book to people across the nation. He felt it was important to get this message to the churches in America right now.

I read through that little book by Francis Frangipane myself and shouted, "That's it!"

I previously had a little revelation about the Jezebel spirit but not anything like I have today. I saw it. This spirit manifests itself just before a fresh prophetic and miracle anointing is getting under way in a church, a home, an organization, a ministry, or a nation. And this spirit of Jezebel must be broken if we're going to move into the greater works that Jesus promised.

Chapter 2

Why Am I Out Of Control?

One evening I preached to a crowd of about 1500. I knew by the Spirit of God that 132 people in that auditorium were being torturously affected by the Jezebel spirit in some way. That was a night of deliverance and divine release.

Some of you reading this have felt controlled, manipulated, and out of control, and you haven't been able to understand why. "Why am I so out of control? Why do I feel so manipulated? Why is this happening this way? Why do I feel like I'm being pushed this way then that way?" This may be *your* day of deliverance!

Others of you reading this book have been doing the manipulating; you have been intimidating others, trying to motivate them through fear or guilt. That spirit is going to be broken from your life if you will humble yourself and repent. You don't want to share in the judgment of those who follow Jezebel and do her bidding.

People may be working for the Jezebel spirit and not even know it.

Jezebel Is Not Necessarily A Female

Even though this spirit is called "Jezebel," it doesn't have a gender. It can strike women or men. The Jezebel spirit brings a deep darkness and deception that can barely, if at all, be discerned by the affected individual. Others may see it, but people with a Jezebel spirit attached to them usually can't recognize it unless there is a humbling of self and an openness of heart to Holy Ghost revelation.

People can say to the controlling, manipulating person, "Look, you're in rebellion. You have this Jezebel spirit of control." But the one with a Jezebel spirit will deny it. That's the dangerous nature of deception. The one being deceived doesn't know it.

Allowing Jezebel To Operate

In Revelation, chapter two, Jesus is speaking to the church in Thyatira.

> And unto the angel of the church in Thyatira write; These things saith the Son of God, who hath his eyes like unto a flame of fire, and his feet *are* like fine brass;
>
> I know thy works, and charity, and service, and faith, and thy patience, and thy works; and the last *to be* more than the first.

Notwithstanding I have a few things against thee, because thou sufferest that woman Jezebel, which calleth herself a prophetess, to teach and to seduce my servants to commit fornication, and to eat things sacrificed unto idols.

And I gave her space to repent of her fornication; and she repented not.

Behold, I will cast her into a bed, and them that commit adultery with her into great tribulation, except they repent of their deeds.

And I will kill her children with death; and all the churches shall know that I am he which searcheth the reins and hearts: and I will give unto every one of you according to your works.

But unto you I say, and unto the rest in Thyatira, as many as have not this doctrine, and which have not known the depths of Satan, as they speak; I will put upon you none other burden.

But that which ye have *already* hold fast till I come.

And he that overcometh, and keepeth my works unto the end, to him will I give power over the nations:

And he shall rule them with a rod of iron; as the vessels of a potter shall they be broken to shivers: even as I received of my Father.

And I will give him the morning star.

He that hath an ear, let him hear what the Spirit saith unto the churches.

—Revelation 2:18-29

Jesus said to His church, "I have a few things against you, because *you allow* that woman Jezebel..." The actual lady He was referring to may or may not have been named Jezebel. What He is doing here is giving us a clue to search out the Scriptures and learn precisely what the name Jezebel means. This woman in Thyatira was operating in the spirit of Jezebel.

Notice, Jezebel has to be "allowed" to operate, and in this case, the pastor was *allowing* Jezebel to function in the church.

He then said, "You allow that woman Jezebel, which calleth herself a prophetess." Notice He didn't say that she *was* a prophetess, but that she was *calling herself* a prophetess. A person can call themselves anything they want to, but it doesn't mean that's what they are. I know people who call themselves "apostles," and they are not.

He said, "You allow her to teach and seduce my servants to commit fornication." He is probably speaking about spiritual fornication; because in Psalm 106, verse 39, God likens idolatry to spiritual fornication.

> **Their evil deeds defiled them, for their love of idols was adultery in the sight of God.**
>
> —**Psalm 106:39 (TLB)**

Jesus continued, "You're seducing My servants to commit fornication." Even if the seduction was not toward physical fornication, He's trying to warn us about the seductive nature of the spirit of Jezebel. Jezebel may seduce a victim into pornography to get control of his life. Jezebel may seduce her victim into a dangerous relationship in order to manipulate their life.

Jesus said, "I gave her space to repent, but she would not." True repentance is foreign to a person with a Jezebel spirit.

We're going to find out what happens to that person who has allowed the spirit of Jezebel to get a foothold.

Jezebel comes into a church and covertly stretches her tentacles of influence and wraps them around as many as she possibly can.

Chapter 3

I Want To Control Things

Let's go back to 1 Kings to find out a little more about this personality called Jezebel. If you look at the life, the style, the character, and the nature of Jezebel in the Bible, you will find the characteristics of the spirit of Jezebel. The devil uses Jezebel to hinder or stall prophetic and miraculous movements of God. He utilizes the Jezebel spirit against young ministers to discourage them and wear them out.

> And Ahab the son of Omri did evil in the sight of the LORD above all that *were* before him.
>
> And it came to pass, as if it had been a light thing for him to walk in the sins of Jeroboam the son of Nebat, that he took to wife Jezebel the daughter of Ethbaal king of the Zidonians, and went and served Baal, and worshipped him.
>
> And he reared up an altar for Baal in the house of Baal, which he had built in Samaria.
>
> And Ahab made a grove; and Ahab did more to provoke the LORD God of Israel to anger than all the kings of Israel that were before him.

> In his days did Hiel the Bethelite build Jericho: he laid the foundation thereof in Abiram his firstborn, and set up the gates thereof in his youngest *son* Segub, according to the word of the LORD, which he spake by Joshua the son of Nun.
>
> —1 Kings 16:30-34

Jezebel married Ahab, a wimpy, whiny king that did more evil in the sight of God than any other king before his time; nonetheless, he was the king. But Jezebel didn't care if he was the king as long as *she* was in control. Now here is the bottom line with Jezebel. A person operating by the spirit of Jezebel has a craving to dominate and to be in control. That person doesn't care if somebody else is king or somebody else is president, as long as "I am in control."

Jezebel Thrives On Control

In a church, a Jezebel spirit doesn't care if somebody else is pastor as long as "she" can be controlling things. She may say, "Well, he's the pastor, but I run the church."

It happened to me back in 1984. For the first time in my life, I thought that I was going to die from stress because I didn't recognize the spirit of Jezebel for what it was. I thought working among Christians would be the grandest thing in the world. We all love God. None of us are self-serving. We just want the will of the Father; that's all. Right?

I have found this is not always the case. A whirl-wind attack against my life manifested just as the church had quadrupled in size and revival was evident. A sense of something big just ahead was in the air.

Then, to my surprise, I discovered rumors going around about me. I couldn't pinpoint their source until God gave me a word of knowledge. It was then that I knew exactly where these vicious lies were coming from, although I couldn't yet prove it objectively. All the confusion, rumors, shifting and shaking going on was happening because somebody else wanted to control the church.

God raises up pastors to be overseers. That means "big picture people." That's what "overseer" means: to see over and above; to see the big picture. God gives only one person this gift of overseeing in any church. Call him the pastor, call him apostle, call him prophet. I don't care what you call him. But *one person*, the overseer of that church, has the oversight of that church and ministry – the big picture from God. He supernaturally sees the whole pie, so to speak. Other people may see a piece of the pie, but the pastor-leader is the only one "gifted" by God to see the big picture. He has to make decisions based on that big picture, not on just a small sliver of the pie.

I wanted God's will for our church, so I fasted for three days and prayed in one of our Sunday school classrooms. God spoke to me during that three-day fast and told me one thing very specifically related to our building program. He said, "Don't go to the bank and borrow money." I was determined to obey.

It wasn't long afterward a man, who I once held in high regard, came to my office to try to convince me to disobey God. I once had a great deal of respect for this man. But now he sat in my office and said, "Look, you're just the pastor. We control the business of the church, and we want you to go to the bank and borrow the money for the building project."

I said, "I'm sorry. I want to be respectful of you; you're an elder, but I've got to obey God."

After that, the threats started coming rapid-fire. This is the nature of a person that has a controlling spirit. They threaten.

"I'm afraid that my family and I are going to have to withhold our tithe until you reconsider," the Jezebel spirit threatened.

I showed him the door, and when I did, it eventually led to a hundred other people going out the door. That's the power of the Jezebel spirit. Jezebel comes into a church and covertly stretches her tentacles of influence and wraps them around as many as she possibly can.

Later in the week, his son came to me in private and said, "I want to talk to you, Pastor." He said. "Look, the problem is that my family has been in control of this church for so long, they feel like they're losing power, and that's why they are acting the way they are."

If his dad ever found out that he came to me secretly, I think that the son would be ostracized from the controlling family (which I not-so-affectionately have named the "Christian Mafia"). I'm at the age where I've decided to be dreadfully truthful even if it hurts. Others said to me, "They are good people in their hearts." Well, I'm not going to say that somebody has a good heart when I know that they're operating in rebellion, wickedness, and evil. I'm not going to say somebody is walking in the Spirit of God when they're operating in the Jezebel spirit.

The son of the controlling patriarch continued, "We've been in control for so long, and the church is growing so fast that we feel like we're getting out of control."

I responded, "Well, that's good. I don't want you or your family to be in control of this church. I don't even want me to be in control. Jesus is the head of this church, and He's the real Chairman of the Board, and if He's the head of the church, He controls the church by speaking to the pastor of the church. He's spoken to me clearly and told me not to go to the bank this time and borrow money. That's that ... period!"

How We Broke Jezebel's Hold

I started conducting morning prayer meetings from 5:30 until 8:30. I'd have my small staff come in and pray with me in the mornings. We didn't know anything about the spirit of Jezebel back then, but we wanted a pure church. So we started binding spirits of control. We had never heard of spiritual warfare at that point; nonetheless, we started binding and casting out "controlling spirits." In my mind, I was thinking they were just ground-level demons, sort of hanging around the rafters. I didn't realize that these demonic creatures were actually attached to people.

Within weeks I started getting dozens of transfer letters. A hundred of them! These people wanted to leave the church and transfer elsewhere. When those controlled by the spirit of Jezebel realized that they were not going to control this pastor, it was too much for them to take. They went elsewhere to try to control another pastor.

After the Jezebels walked out the door, along with those they influenced, our church income immediately went up by nearly 30 percent even though they had threatened that the church wouldn't survive without "their tithe." Not only that, our growing church started growing even faster, and we were able to build our new 3000-seat church facility without ever borrowing money from the bank.

The bottom line of this spirit of Jezebel is that she *has to* control. Please remember, I'm only referring to "she" because Jezebel is a feminine name. Evil spirits have no gender and can just as easily attach themselves to males as well as females.

The Jezebel spirit may manifest in a wife who feels, "I've got to control my husband."

The Jezebel spirit may manifest in a husband who thinks, "I've got to control my wife." It doesn't matter if it's through the means of intimidation, fear, guilt, or some kind of manipulation; those with a Jezebel spirit have to control.

Evangelist Experiences Jezebel Deacons

Evangelist Ken Gaub was preaching at a particular church for a pastor when he got a phone call at his hotel.

A man's voice said, "I just talked to the pastor. I'm supposed to pick you up for lunch at noon."

The pastor hadn't mentioned anything about it to Ken; nonetheless, he went downstairs and waited for his ride. A man arrived and drove the evangelist to a restaurant where a private room had been reserved. When they walked in, there were six or seven others waiting around the table.

Ken noticed that the pastor wasn't there so he asked, "Where's the pastor?"

"We don't know where he is," a spokesman responded, as if he had been expecting the pastor to be present. Ken felt something was amiss, yet chatted as if everything was fine. But in his spirit, he felt some kind of reservation, as if something was out of order. He went ahead and ate with the men, all the while trying to figure out what was going on.

Finally, after the last cup of coffee was served and the plates were cleared, a man closed the door to the private room. The spokesman began, "Ken, the reason we've called you here is because we've got some things against our pastor, and we're thinking about asking him to leave. These men around this table comprise the official board of our church. We'd like you to consider being our pastor. What would you think about that?"

Ken now knew why he had such an unsettled feeling in his spirit the entire time.

"First of all," Ken replied disgustedly, "if I were to take over the church, my first order of business would be to fire this board and replace it with godly men. You men have demonstrated the lowest ethical standards I can imagine by having a meeting like this behind the pastor's back. Secondly ..."

Just then, he was interrupted. "Well, wait a minute, Ken. We aren't asking you to *take over*. We are just asking you to be the pastor."

No, they weren't asking him to *take over* because they wanted to be in charge themselves and needed the pastor to be their puppet. Ken told them he was the pastor's friend and would have to let the pastor know what was going on behind his back.

Jezebels. Look at the tactics.

First, the man used deception to get Ken to the lunch table. "I just talked with the pastor. I'm supposed to pick you up for lunch." He probably hadn't talked to the pastor, and if he did, he certainly didn't say anything about lunch. The Jezebelian deacon used deception. When Ken asked where the pastor was, they responded that they didn't know, as if the pastor was supposed to be there. Deceptive words, deceptive vocal tones, deceptive body language was used.

Second, for a board to have a meeting without the pastor's knowledge, is probably a violation of the church by-laws, and if not, it's certainly a clear violation of common ethical standards. But Jezebels have no regard for authority whether it's constitutional authority, ethical or moral authority, or people in authority.

Third, they didn't want a pastor that would "take over." Of course not, Jezebel is the one who craves control. A Jezebelian deacon wants a pastor who will mind his own business, be a little chaplain on Sundays, and let Jezebel run the church.

Every day in America and the world, you'll find a pastor somewhere that can't understand why everything seems to be out of control. Why are people leaving the church? Why is there confusion? Why do I feel like such a failure? The answer may be as close as your board room.

Jezebel teaches that deacons are elected to represent the people to the pastor. The Bible teaches that deacons are *selected* to represent the pastor to the people and to be helpers for the man of God (Acts 6). Jezebel teaches that the board runs the church, lays the vision, makes the policies, and runs the "show." The Bible teaches that God raises up *a man*, a pastor, to be the overseer, responsible and accountable to God for following Christ's mandate for His Church. A Jezebel deacon will always want to play the role of devil's advocate anytime the pastor tries to share his vision or heart beat.

I faced my share of deacon Jezebels the first four or five years of my ministry in the church. Thankfully, I haven't had a Jezebel board member since those early days. I have godly, loving deacons and elders who understand their biblical roles and help me to care for the flock of God. As a result, our church keeps growing, prospering, and making disciples for Jesus Christ.

She Hates True Prophets

Jezebel killed the true prophets of God. She's still at work today trying to kill the faith, enthusiasm, and growth of true men and women of God.

The historic Jezebel had her own wimpy prophets who would say and do what she wanted them to. She brought in prophets to her table; prophets that would do what she wanted them to do. Jezebel loves to be around people in spiritual authority *as long as she can influence and control them.*

She said, "Prophets, I'm in control, and I'll tell you what to say, and I'll tell you what to do. You just be like little chaplains around here, but I'm going to be in charge."

She had the security of 450 prophets of Baal and another 400 prophets of Ashteroth around her table. She then went about systematically killing the true prophets of God.

Today, the spirit of Jezebel doesn't actually stab or cut off the heads of the true prophets, but through innuendo, through slander, gossip, and rebellion, she endeavors to "kill" the true prophets of God.

A person with a Jezebel spirit often appears to be very religious. After all, she has her very own religious prophets. It is of no concern to her that these prophets are not prophets of God but prophets of religion. She loves religion but hates true prophets.

When my book, *The World Beyond,* was released, we decided to give everyone in our community a free copy. It's a book all about Heaven and how to get there according to the Bible. In one day, we distributed 89,000 copies, and during the course of a few other days, 11,000 more were distributed, making it 100,000 copies given away free to people in our city and in some of the surrounding townships.

The testimonies that followed were amazing. An 82-year-old woman accepted Jesus Christ after all these years. Hundreds of "sinners" came to a free dinner we sponsored where they met Jesus Christ in a personal way. Calls of support and thanks flooded our office.

At the same time, calls of complaint also came to our office from people clearly bound by the religious Jezebel spirit.

"I belong to _____ church, and I don't appreciate the garbage you are distributing."

"I'm a religious person and think it's terrible that you are telling people there is only one way to Heaven. There are a lot more ways to Heaven than just through Jesus."

"I am a _____ and have been since I was born. And that book is just a bunch of cr***!"

You see, Jezebel wants to control the city and the minds of the people. She'll use religion, manipulation, or coercion; it doesn't matter as long as she is in control. The Jezebel of the Bible surrounded herself with false religious prophets and killed the true prophets of God.

Those whom Jezebel influences will stand before God one day to answer for what they have said and done. Their homes will come under a curse in this life, as Jezebel's home came under a curse. It was terrible how Jezebel ended up, as we shall see later.

The bottom line is control.
Jezebel has to control.

Chapter 4

False Prophets

Why are there so many pastoral drop-outs today? It is, at least partly, because this spirit of intimidation and control brings a terrible discouragement to pastors. You've heard of people going from church to church, ruining pastor after pastor? Some people seem to be professional controllers. "I've got to have the pastor's time. I've got to have the pastor's ear or the pastor's this or that."

I'm just glad that I've been through it and had good people like my wife and my prayer partners who held up my arms and helped me survive. Facing the Jezebel spirit early in my ministry has helped me to have a more discerning eye.

Oppression In The Church

On one particular occasion, our church service seemed to have some kind of oppression in it. Have you ever noticed that some services are vibrant, the

Spirit of God is moving, everybody is happy, and there's so much joy, and in other services, there's some manner of reserve or oppression? Well, I was on the platform, and under my breath I was binding the unidentifiable spirit of oppression. I couldn't identify it precisely for some reason, but at the end of the service I went back to the narthex, and a beautiful lady, all dolled up, walked up to me and said, "Hello, Pastor, I want you to know that my name is Kay, and I'm a prophetess."

Buzzers started going off in my spirit. "Buzz, buzz buzz…"

I replied, "You are, huh?"

She arrogantly continued, "Yes, I am, and I see you announced that you have a missionary trip going to Venezuela. You have to stop it."

"Why?" I inquired.

"Because ten of the people going on the trip will be killed by terrorists," Kay insisted.

"Oh?" I questioned cautiously.

"Yes, and you're going to know that I'm a prophetess because an earthquake is coming to this city before December 13th."

I simply said, "Thank you, but not knowing you, I cannot accept your prophecies," and I walked away and wrote down what she had said.

I prayed seriously about the trip to Venezuela, and God's word to my heart was "Go." So our team went on the Venezuelan mission trip. When they returned, they reported that it was one of the most successful missions trips ever.

A False Prophetess

Shortly after my encounter with her, I received a letter from Kay, the one who *called herself* a prophetess. It read: "My son, I am now going to have to bring you home before your time because you refuse to accept my servant as a true prophetess." The entire letter was one big death threat from God that "could not be reversed *unless*" I recognized this woman as His prophetess.

Remember Jesus said that Jezebel *called herself* a prophetess? Kay *called herself* a prophetess, although she had no credible evidence and certainly no spiritual fruit.

December 13th came and went, and there was no earthquake.

I'm always cautious when somebody calls themselves a prophet or prophetess. They may be a prophet, but I'll know it by their accuracy, character, and fruit.

We have some genuine prophets in our church. I believe there is a man that, every once in awhile, will call me with a prophetic message that is confirming and accurate. If he sees me in the hall, he'll sometimes give me an encouraging prophetic message. I believe in prophets. I just don't accept false prophets or people who *call themselves* prophets who do nothing but se-duce God's servants into confusion, bad decisions, sen-suality, or licentiousness.

Jezebel called herself a prophetess. In reality she worshipped Ashteroth, the god of licentiousness and sexuality. She also worshipped Baal, an agricultural god named "the son of the dragon." Now if that doesn't tip you off, by knowing what god she's serving, I don't know what will. The bottom line, once again, is control. Jezebel has to control.

So, she kills the true prophets or slanders them, just as the "prophetess" Kay told me, in a "letter from God" that God was going to take me home before my time because I would not receive His servant, the prophet-ess Kay, as a true prophetess.

I wrote her back, incidentally, and said:

> I do accept you as a "prophetess," Kay. I *do* believe you are a prophetess – a false prophetess.

> Sincerely,
>
> Pastor Williams

Chapter 5

Exceeding Authority

The Jezebel spirit thinks nothing of exceeding her authority and using the king's name to do it.

> And Jezebel his wife said unto him, Dost thou now govern the kingdom of Israel? arise, *and* eat bread, and let thine heart be merry: I will give thee the vineyard of Naboth the Jezreelite.

> So she wrote letters in Ahab's name, and sealed *them* with his seal, and sent the letters unto the elders and to the nobles that *were* in his city, dwelling with Naboth.

> And she wrote in the letters, saying, Proclaim a fast, and set Naboth on high among the people:

> And set two men, sons of Belial, before him, to bear witness against him, saying, Thou didst blaspheme God and the king. And *then* carry him out, and stone him, that he may die.

> And the men of his city, *even* the elders and the nobles who were the inhabitants in his city, did as Jezebel had sent unto them, *and* as it *was* written in the letters which she had sent unto them.

> They proclaimed a fast, and set Naboth on high among the people.
>
> And there came in two men, children of Belial, and sat before him: and the men of Belial witnessed against him, *even* against Naboth, in the presence of the people, saying, Naboth did blaspheme God and the king. Then they carried him forth out of the city, and stoned him with stones, that he died.
>
> Then they sent to Jezebel, saying, Naboth is stoned, and is dead.
>
> —1 Kings 21:7-14

Here's the story: there was a man named Naboth who owned a little vineyard. King Ahab loved that little piece of real estate, so he went to Naboth and asked him if he'd sell the property. Naboth replied, "Oh, no, King. I really want this property." Let me put it in my amplified paraphrase, "I'm saving this for my retirement; I'm going to build a little house on this property someday." The king went home and pouted. That led to depression. He really wanted that property, and he couldn't get it. So he pouted like an immature brat that didn't get a toy he wanted.

While he was pouting, Jezebel walked in.

"You wimp, what's wrong with you? Why don't you just take the property from him? After all, you're the king," Jezebel snipped.

Jezebel Exceeds Her Authority

Remember, she doesn't care if he's the king as long as she's in control. So, without Ahab's approval or knowledge, she went out and wrote a decree in the king's name, stamped it with his personal seal, sent it out, and ordered the death of Naboth, the man who owned that vacant property. She exceeded her authority, saying it was in the name of the king. So the decree went out, and the king's men killed Naboth. Jezebel proudly took possession of the small vineyard lot and said to Ahab, "There's your piece of real estate; now be happy."

"Well, how did you do this?" the king inquired.

"Never mind, it's none of your business. I'm in control here."

She may not have actually said these words, but this is the nature of Jezebel. "I've got to control. I can't simply motivate you by love; I've got to manipulate you." It's like some sick game.

Jezebel far exceeds her authority. You find this spirit in some employees who have been around for a long time and feel they know better than the boss.

It's like the associate minister or business administrator in a church who makes independent decisions the pastor knows nothing about. In business, I believe many executives have suffered and been brought down because of unauthorized decisions made by others on their behalf.

Unfortunately, there are even some pastors who operate in the spirit of Jezebel. They try to make people feel that coming to their church is compulsory or man-datory and that other churches are substandard. They use guilt or intimidation to manipulate their members.

You can come to church and be under a pastor's protection, but if you want to step out from under it, you can do that too. As a pastor, I am not keeping chains with fifteen-pound balls on people here.

Jezebel's Characteristics

The spirit of Jezebel sees people as pawns, not as living human beings that have feelings, dreams, de-sires, goals, needs, and wants. If she can use them and then get rid of them, she'll do it.

She's fiercely independent and vicious for preemi-nence and control, and she consistently, though often covertly, rebels against any constituted authority. She has to dominate and control. The only time this spirit will appear to be submissive or servant-like is when she hopes to gain some strategic advantage.

This spirit, as I have previously mentioned, is with-out gender – it may be attached to either a male or a female. The most susceptible to the Jezebel spirit are those who allow insecurity, jealousy, vanity, or ambi-tion to govern their lives. For example, if there is a wife who fantasizes about having a more spiritual hus-band, she becomes very susceptible to the Jezebel spirit, and it will bring a curse upon her home. Or she may fantasize about a more spiritual husband, but it's not the one she's married to.

When she sees some man praying at a prayer meeting or involved in spiritual things at the church and says, "If only my husband were spiritual like that, if my husband were just a little stronger," she starts fantasizing about another man who may appear to be stronger and more spiritual than her husband. She is getting close to the seduction of Jezebel. And if she attaches Jezebel to her life, she is in deep trouble.

Another example is when a man is unable to control his wife. He wants to dominate and control. He'll say, "You're supposed to submit to me." He uses Bible verses to put guilt upon his wife, and when he can't change her or control her through his manipulative tactics, he goes to his place of employment and tries to manipulate the people there to make up for the lack of control he has over his wife. He becomes susceptible to the Jezebel spirit.

There are all kinds of examples. I'd like you to read Francis Frangipane's book on the Jezebel spirit. You can read it in an hour or less.

Again, I can't emphasize it enough. *A person with the spirit of Jezebel has to dominate. Control is what the spirit of Jezebel craves.*

Judas Iscariot craved to be in charge. "I've got to be in charge of the money. That way I can control it and take a little bit now and then." Later Judas thought something like this, "I don't like the way things are going in the ministry of Jesus, so I'm going to cash in now and get some benefits while I can. Maybe I can force Jesus to expose His Messianic powers to the rest of the world. Then we'll get this kingdom thing on the roll."

Judas had to be in control. He couldn't just let God do things in His time. He had to control, manipulate, maneuver, and use covert tactics and strategies to try to force Jesus to do something Jesus wasn't ready to do. The very thing he wanted, power and control, he lost. All of the other disciples stayed with Jesus and ended up receiving astonishing power on the day of Pentecost. You talk about having control. They had control over demon spirits, over sickness and disease. What Judas craved, he lost. While those who submitted to God's will and timing were filled with power from another world, Judas was already dead and stationed in Hell for eternity.

What a high price tag the Jezebel spirit carries.

Chapter 6

Maneuvering Into Position

The Jezebel spirit seeks to maneuver into leadership positions or inside positions in ministries such as intercessory prayer. "She *calls herself* a prophetess." Remember, Jezebel craves and feeds upon recognition.

Jezebelian Intercessors

The pastor at one of our branch churches went through a Jezebelian situation right after the September 11, 2001, terrorist attack on America. One of his key intercessors said to the pastor, "I've heard from God, Pastor, and the attack on the World Trade Center was the judgment of God on America."

The pastor responded sharply, "No, it was not! Like Pastor Dave says, it has the fingerprints of the devil. They *stole* airplanes, they *killed* people, and they *destroyed* buildings. That is the devil, not God." (John 10:10)

America is still the greatest nation on earth, in spite of all the sin in this nation that God hates. We are still the nation with the largest number of professing believers. The largest prayer networks are right here in the United States of America. The attack on America in 2001 by terrorists was not God's judgment.

God is not mad at America; God loves this nation. It was not God's judgment; it was the devil. It was terrorism. If you say that it was God's judgment, then you have to say that it was the god of those terrorists who brought the judgment. That makes you a follower of a different god than the One we read about in the Bible. If you believe God brought down the World Trade Center buildings in that terrorist attack on America in September of 2001, then you believe in the wrong god.

So the pastor, even though this was the leading intercessor, said to her, "No, it was not God's judgment; it was the devil."

This "I've got to control" type of intercessor was offended that the pastor didn't accept her imagined "word from the Lord," so she started passing out typewritten sheets with her prophecies to people in the congregation. People can read things like that if they want to, and they can pick up a Jezebel spirit if they want, but I'm not going to. I'm going to discern the spirits and see if they are of God. I'm going to test the spirits and see whether they are of God.

Beloved, believe not every spirit, but try the spirits whether they are of God: because many false prophets are gone out into the world.

—1 John 4:1

Some things sound right, but you get a strange feeling and suspect something just isn't right about this. You're testing the spirits.

As it turned out, there was a big blow up in the church. They lost a board member and a few other people who identified with the Jezebelian intercessor. It's like the tail of Leviathan — the tail of the devil that flung stars out of Heaven. The "tail" of Jezebel tries to fling stars out of a church.

Again, the bottom line is that Jezebel wants to control your life, your pastor, your business, your family, and your church.

Elijah Represents God's Interests
Jezebel Represents Satan's Interests

Elijah, a true prophet of God and a contemporary of Jezebel, represents God's interests. Jezebel represents the spirit trying to block God's interests. Elijah was opposed by Jezebel. John the Baptist came in the "spirit and power of Elijah" and called people to repent just as Elijah years earlier called people to humble themselves and repent. Just as Jezebel hated Elijah, Herodias hated John the Baptist. Herodias, in the spirit of Jezebel, thwarted John's efforts and eventually had him murdered. She had the same spirit as the original Jezebel. When John the Baptist came, Jesus said he had come in the "spirit and power of Elijah." Remember, Elijah represents the interests of God. Thus, John represented God's interests, and Satan raised up another Jezebel. Herodias, the king's wife, possessed with the Jezebel spirit, used her control to manipulate her husband into making a deal that ended in the execution of John.

But before that, Herodias had John the Baptist so discouraged that he didn't even know any longer if Jesus was the Messiah. He sent a message, "Are you the One we are looking for, or should we look for someone else?" Just as Elijah became discouraged when threatened by Jezebel, John was now discouraged by the threats of Herodias, a woman possessed with the Jezebel spirit.

Jezebel will never humble herself. In Jezebel there is no repentance. Jezebel enjoys wild confusion, as you saw in her prophets out there yelling and screaming, having their prayer meeting, trying to get their gods to answer. That's when humble Elijah, God's real man, just sat back and watched. Finally he laughed and asked, "Why don't you wait awhile? Your god might be out on the toilet, or maybe he's sleeping right now."

Jezebel tried to discourage Elijah, even threatened him. That's a characteristic of Jezebel. People that have the Jezebel spirit will frequently resort to threats when things don't go the way they think they should. They'll get to the threat sooner or later.

The Greater Works Generation

In the last chapter of Malachi, God promises to send Elijah before the Lord's coming. This means that we are on the brink of being a part of another "Greater Works Generation." Yes, I believe you and I are this Greater Works Generation. The spirit and power of Elijah is penetrating this generation of Bible-believing, Christ-loving, Christ-exalting, Spirit-filled believers. The Spirit of Elijah has God's interests at heart, not self-interests. We are seeing it in young and old people alike.

> **Behold, I will send you Elijah the prophet before the coming of the great and dreadful day of the LORD:**
>
> —Malachi 4:5

As the Greater Works Generation, we are going to flow in an unparalleled prophetic anointing. We are going to flow in a fresh, miraculous anointing. The devil has no prophetic abilities, but he sees it coming, so he has sent spirits of Jezebel, hoping to stop it through control, manipulation, threats, and fear.

Later in this book, I'm going to show you exactly how Jezebel tries to control people's lives. You'll be able to identify that spirit in an instant and rebuke it.

Three Things Jezebel Hates

There are three things the Jezebel spirit hates and cannot resist: humility, repentance, and people who stand up to her boldly. One of my prayer confessions practically every day is, "God, without you I can do nothing. Unless You build the house, I labor in vain." That's been the cornerstone for everything I do. I never want to think that I'm somebody more special or more holy than other precious believers. I know that if I were to leave my church tomorrow, it would have no more effect in the long run than pulling your hand out of the ocean. The vision that God has put upon my heart for this church and this community is so big, is so huge, that what I see compared to where we are, makes me feel like somewhat of a failure. I want to stay that way.

If you ever hear me talking about how great, wonderful, and holy I am and I start beating church members up verbally for all their little sins, look out, there's a Jezebel in the pulpit. Mary Jo, my wife, knows me. She sees me every day. She knows I have feet of clay, not steel. And the Bible says, "If any man thinks he stands, let him take heed lest he fall."

> **Wherefore let him that thinketh he standeth take heed lest he fall.**
>
> **—1 Corinthians 10:12**

Jezebel Is 'Never Wrong'

Jezebel rarely admits that she is wrong unless it has a strategic advantage in her scheme of manipulation. I encourage pastors to share not only their victories, but also their failures. It helps to keep us humble and helps people relate to us. It keeps us from developing a spirit of Jezebel.

To expose my own frailty, I'll tell you what I did one time. I was very upset with one of our employees, and I exploded. In frustration, I threw a Mont Blanc pen; I yelled and screamed. I pushed him; I went into his office and knocked a hole in the wall, I was so mad. Ten minutes later I was begging his forgiveness saying, "This was so wrong, not just for a man of God but for a Christian!" And I asked, "Will you forgive me?" I repented within ten minutes.

Jezebel can't say, "I repent" and then be specific about it. Jezebel can't respond to an altar call unless it's for a mere show in order to manipulate someone. Jezebel can't say, "I was wrong." Jezebel just can't do it. If you're controlled by the spirit of Jezebel when an altar call is given, you can't get out of your seat and get up there. You think, "Oh, somebody is going to think that I've done something that I haven't done because I'm almost perfect." Jezebel hates humility. The Jezebel spirit hates repentance.

You see, you can have all your false prophets of Baal around yelling and screaming, wiggling, and crying, and barking like dogs and think you're in revival. Elijah was calling the nation to repentance because he wanted *true revival*. John the Baptist was calling people to repentance because he wanted *true revival*. This Spirit that God is pouring out in this day, giving us the attitude and power of Elijah, is calling for repentance.

I became angry at our accounting lady one time. I don't even remember what she said that angered me, but I remember that I started yelling at her, and I kicked a wastebasket across the room. Then I fired her. Ten minutes later I hired her back and begged her to forgive me for my carnal temperamental display. I wish I could say that I'm perfect, but I'm not. I wish God didn't ask me to share these things with you, but He has, and I'm telling you this to say something important to you.

God does not expect you to be perfect but to *be quick to repent*. ***Be quick to repent.*** Don't hold things in. When you hold things in, you make yourself susceptible to the deception of Jezebel. Let me tell you, once you're in the grip of the Jezebel spirit, the consequences are awful, as we shall learn later.

Jezebel hates people who are becoming more Christlike. You see, Jesus Christ always motivates by love. Jezebel does not understand that. Jezebel has to motivate by manipulation, intimidation, guilt, or fear, making it compulsory that you act on her wishes ... or else! Jesus Christ motivates by love, and so do those who really love and serve Him.

If you have been living a life that is manipulated, intimidated, and you've been living in fear, you need deliverance. Faith can't operate in the same place where fear is. This generation, the generation of turning impossibilities into realities, this generation of greater works, is going to have to go forth without fear. Jezebel will say that if you do, the devil's going to come against your house. Tell him to get behind you. Set him down in the Name of Jesus and with the Word of God.

Don't Take It Anymore!

You have to stand up to the spirit of Jezebel. You have to decide that *you're not going to take it anymore*. You also have to come in repentance and humility if you want to have power over the spirit of Jezebel. The Jezebel spirit will not back down until you stand up to it. I promise you, God will give you enough power to defeat Jezebel.

I know you want to be a part of this "Greater Works Generation," and you're not going to let the spirit of a sensual, licentious, unspiritual, wicked queen stop you. You are going forward, not backward.

A person with a Jezebel spirit is obsessed with power.

Chapter 7

Jezebel Discourages

The devil employs an army of demonic forces, principalities, powers, rulers of darkness, and spiritual wickedness in high places. This, of course, would include the Jezebel spirit.

> **For we wrestle not against flesh and blood, but against principalities, against powers, against the rulers of the darkness of this world, against spiritual wickedness in high *places*.**
>
> **—Ephesians 6:12**

Active on and around the earth are various ranks of demonic creatures ranging from ground-level demons to strategic principalities, all with the evil design of hindering and hurting the Church of Jesus Christ and redirecting believers from their simple devotion to Jesus Christ. One of those powerful, strategic spirits is Jezebel.

Let me remind you again that when we speak of Jezebel, we're not speaking of a spirit that is gender specific. In other words, when we refer to Jezebel as "she," we are not saying the demon is a female. Demons have no gender. Spirits are neither male nor female, but they can influence either male or female. We are speaking of a spirit that *can* have influence through a female but can *also* have influence through a male. Jezebel doesn't care if she uses a male or a female. Again, the reason I refer to Jezebel as a "she" is because the characteristics of this spirit called Jezebel are the characteristics of a woman in the Bible also called Jezebel.

The Need For Power

A person with a Jezebel spirit is obsessed with power. She thrives on the power of controlling people's lives. She has no real power or authority except that which her victims allow her. Jezebel is a power hungry demon. She encourages spiritual idolatry and adultery while maintaining a place in the Christian Church. She thinks nothing of exceeding her authority for self-serving reasons, usurping authority, usually covertly.

A Jezebelian Pastor

The pastor of one of our affiliate churches asked me to co-sign for his church's refinancing some years ago. I had already been getting some discernment on the pastor of that church but couldn't put my finger on any specific issues. I went to the closing to guarantee that payments would be made to the bank. I read over the paperwork and was shocked to discover that it had been drawn up in a way that named this pastor and his group on the property deed but named me and my church as the ones responsible for payments.

I looked at that paperwork and said, "Wait a minute. Wait a minute right now." I looked at the bank vice president and said, "Ron, this puts their name on the deed instead of our name on the deed. If we're putting over a hundred thousand dollars on the line, we want our name on the deed until it's paid off. We are always named on the deeds of our church properties." I then asked him who instructed him to fill out the paperwork like this. He looked over at the pastor of that church and said, "He did." I quickly responded, "I'm not going to sign this."

Later we were told that the pastor had been planning for months to defect and had laid out a careful, strategic plan to legally take our church and property, leaving us with the responsibility to pay for it all.

We learned later this hireling pastor had a Jezebel spirit — a spirit of control. People would come to us saying things like, "I don't know why, but I feel so intimidated around him, I feel so threatened by him, I feel like he's controlling my life." The people that came under his Jezebel control have now lost control of their lives, and they can't get away. This is typical of how cults operate. They bring you under their control, and it's hard to break loose. This is the Jezebel spirit.

Independent, ambitious for preeminence, rebellious against spiritual authority, she has to dominate and control your life, or she's not happy.

The Jezebel spirit loves to maneuver its way into leadership positions, insisting on recognition, and usually covertly but sometimes overtly, opposes true spiritual authority and power.

Jezebel Discourages True Men And Women Of God

The Jezebel spirit thrives on spreading discouragement to true men of God. Elijah had just had a great miracle of God, and word was sent to him from Jezebel that she was going to have his head on a platter.

Here was Elijah, this great prophet of God, anointed of God to do marvelous miracles and great works, and when this little pip-squeak of a woman, Jezebel, threatened, "I'm going to have your head on a platter," he ran scared. He hid under a juniper tree, feeling sorry for himself, saying, "I'm worthless, I'm no good, what good am I anyway." He was responsible earlier for calling fire out of Heaven to devour an offering to God, humiliating 850 false prophets. Now he's running discouraged and depressed.

Please, never say or do anything to discourage a preacher especially after he preaches or ministers. That's the time when the devil is all over him anyway telling him what a lousy job he did. If ten people were saved, he thinks it should have been twenty. He's fighting off these demons who are telling him how bad he is.

Immediately after a church service is the easiest time to discourage a preacher. I had to put up with it for almost four years. A guy came up to me every time without fail, and if it wasn't on Sunday, he'd make sure to drop by the office on Monday or Tuesday to let me know everything I did wrong. It's no wonder that so many pastors leave the pastorate and go into secular employment to sell insurance or something else, because this spirit works hard to bring discouragement to men of God.

Here was Elijah, the man of God, discouraged.

John the Baptist came in the spirit and power of Elijah, and there was another Jezebel spirit who was in Herodias. John the Baptist was calling for repentance, the one thing Jezebel really hates. Jezebel will apologize, if necessary, if it will serve her purposes, but you will never see her repent, because she hates true repentance. She hates it when people draw close to God.

Herodias, influenced by the Jezebel spirit, had John the Baptist put in prison. John started doubting himself. Here was John the Baptist who pointed to Jesus and said, "Behold the Lamb of God who takes away the sin of the world!" Jesus was baptized by John. John said, "I'm not worthy to baptize You; You should be baptizing me." And he said, "I'm not worthy to even loose His sandal. This is the One who will baptize You with the Holy Ghost."

Now he is in prison, he is discouraged, he is depressed. He sends word to Jesus, "Are you really the one, or should we look for another to come?"

Jezebel, in these last days, is the spirit that will try to discourage believers from flowing in that greater works ministry, in the spirit and power of Elijah, that God promised would take place before the coming of the Lord.

> **See, I will send you the prophet Elijah before that great and dreadful day of the LORD comes.**
>
> **—Malachi 4:5 (NIV)**

The spirit of Jezebel has to be broken.

Chapter 8

Jezebel's Witchcraft

The Jezebel spirit grows and thrives in confusion and lack of peace. Now why is there confusion?

In II Kings when Jehu was asked by Jezebel's son about peace, he responded, "What peace? So long as the whoredoms of thy mother Jezebel and her witchcrafts are so many."

> And it came to pass, when Joram saw Jehu, that he said, *Is it* peace, Jehu? And he answered, What peace, so long as the whoredoms of thy mother Jezebel and her witchcrafts *are so* many?
>
> —2 Kings 9:22

There was no peace, no order, as long as Jezebel's witchcraft was at work.

Confusion

Have you ever faced absolute confusion? You don't know why somebody said something, but it just haunts you. It confuses you, and you can't make sense of it. If you face something like that, I can guarantee there was some form of witchcraft involved because that's the way witchcraft works.

Witchcraft, according to Galatians 5:19-21, starts out as a work of the flesh. Witchcraft, white magic, or otherwise is basically a way to control and manipulate other people, whether it's through fear, guilt, or other methods. It is the spirit of Jezebel. Jezebel used witchcraft. Once you begin using witchcraft by trying to control and manipulate other people, you begin to attract those kinds of demons that bring confusion, frustration, and lack of peace.

God is not the author of confusion. The devil, the father of lies, is the author of confusion, and that is why you seem confused and uncomfortable when you are being manipulated. You can ask, "Why?" a thousand times and never get the answer. Why? Because witchcraft has been released against you.

What Is Witchcraft?

The Scripture says that Jezebel's witchcrafts were many. What exactly is witchcraft? It is the *desire to control other people* through manipulations, incantations, etc. If you're in the flesh, you're thinking, "I've got to control my wife; I've got to control her, and if I can't control her, I'm not going to be happy." Or "I've got to control my husband. If I can't control the way he thinks and can't control what he does, then I'll do something to control him. I'll quit talking, or I'll say something that will hurt him really bad." Or the husband may withhold compliments or say something sarcastic with the goal of manipulating.

If you have to manipulate, whether it's people or situations, then what will happen is that you're going to attract those kinds of demons. You will then enter the realm of demonic witchcraft. You're going to bring demons into your home. It's no wonder the home of Jezebel became cursed and Jesus said her children will be killed with death. It happened to the original Jezebel.

> And unto the angel of the church in Thyatira write; These things saith the Son of God, who hath his eyes like unto a flame of fire, and his feet *are* like fine brass;
>
> I know thy works, and charity, and service, and faith, and thy patience, and thy works; and the last *to be* more than the first.
>
> Notwithstanding I have a few things against thee, because thou sufferest that woman Jezebel, which calleth herself a prophetess, to teach and to seduce my servants to commit fornication, and to eat things sacrificed unto idols.
>
> And I gave her space to repent of her fornication; and she repented not.
>
> Behold, I will cast her into a bed, and them that commit adultery with her into great tribulation, except they repent of their deeds.
>
> And I will kill her children with death...
>
> —Revelation 2:18-23a

You see, the reason there is so much confusion when Jezebel is active is because her so-called "truth" is corrupt. She brings deception, confusion, and agitation.

Suppose it is a hot August day and I say, "Here, have a glass of iced tea." You say, "Oh bless you, Pastor Dave! This is great." But if I had poison in that iced tea, and it was 99 percent fresh iced tea but 1 percent poison, you would *not* say, "Bless you, Pastor Dave." You would say, "Pastor Dave is worthy of a curse over his home."

We remember the so-called Reverend Jim Jones who put poison in people's drinks back in the 1970s. You say that man is cursed. Well, the same is true when Jezebel spreads her deception. There is confusion. Why? It's because Jezebel flows in an atmosphere of fear, insecurity, conflict, and confusion. Her "truth" is mixed with deceptions.

Her House Was Cursed

Now what happened to Jezebel's family? Her whole family came under a curse because she would not repent. I Kings 21:20-25 talks about this curse.

> And Ahab said to Elijah, Hast thou found me, O mine enemy? And he answered, I have found *thee*: because thou hast sold thyself to work evil in the sight of the LORD.
>
> Behold, I will bring evil upon thee, and will take away thy posterity, and will cut off from Ahab him that pisseth against the wall, and him that is shut up and left in Israel,
>
> And will make thine house like the house of Jeroboam the son of Nebat, and like the house of Baasha the son of Ahijah, for the provocation wherewith thou hast provoked *me* to anger, and made Israel to sin.
>
> And of Jezebel also spake the LORD, saying, The dogs shall eat Jezebel by the wall of Jezreel.

> Him that dieth of Ahab in the city the dogs shall
> eat; and him that dieth in the field shall the fowls
> of the air eat.
>
> But there was none like unto Ahab, which did
> sell himself to work wickedness in the sight of
> the LORD, whom Jezebel his wife stirred up.
>
> —1 Kings 21:20-25

Even though King Ahab eventually humbled himself somewhat, Jezebel never did. As a result, a curse came upon their son, "...but in his son's days will I bring evil upon his house" (I Kings 21:29c).

Notice back in Revelation, chapter two, that Jezebel seduces true servants of God. Jesus says the church was *allowing* this woman, Jezebel, who *calls herself* a prophetess, to teach and seduce his servants. Servants of Jesus, listen to me. It is possible to be seduced by the Jezebel spirit. Jesus Himself said it, and He was not happy with the pastor who was allowing the spirit of Jezebel to seduce His servants.

You are His servants, not my servants. I am here, placed by God as a pastor, to feed you, to oversee the flock, to be an example for you, and to protect you. Any pastor that allows the Jezebel spirit in the organization is just as bad as a person who would give you a glass of iced tea with 1 percent of deadly poison in it. Jezebel seduces. She has a seducing nature.

Remember, St. Paul warned about seducing spirits.

> Now the Spirit speaketh expressly, that in the latter times some shall depart from the faith, giving heed to seducing spirits, and doctrines of devils;
>
> Speaking lies in hypocrisy; having their conscience seared with a hot iron.
>
> —1 Timothy 4:1-2

You see, Jezebel loves to control people, but before she can control, she has to seduce. She draws her strength from power and control. She loves getting on church boards and places where there are unscriptural systems of government. I'm convinced that Jezebel is on more boards and committees in churches than any other spirit from the dark kingdom of the devil.

Jezebel Seduces Often With Flattery

How does she seduce? One way is with flattery. I've come to identify Jezebel spirits pretty quickly. There was a man who came to Mount Hope Church and caught me after the service. He said, "I have to tell you something, Pastor. The holy anointing was all over you today. I have never in my life seen anyone more anointed than you. In fact, as I was looking into the spirit world, I saw rain coming down out of Heaven on you as you preached."

Now if I hadn't been in the Spirit at that moment, I might have taken his words seriously. Instead, when he said it, there was something sickening going on inside of me. I knew there was some unclean spirit present in his words. Everybody loves a sincere compliment. There is nothing wrong with that. Everybody appreciates a genuine compliment, but flattery is what the anti-Christ is going to use for the sake of controlling world leaders.

> With flattery he will corrupt those who have violated the covenant, but the people who know their God will firmly resist him.
>
> —Daniel 11:32 (NIV)

Well, it turns out that this flattering fellow who saw "rain coming out of Heaven" simply wanted to worm his way into the church in order to gain control.

Jezebel spirits love to have the attention of the pastor and key leaders. I'm thankful to God that I was able to discern it from the start. What's harder for me to discern, however, is when I've had a relationship with somebody, we've prayed together and done a lot of things together. When the Jezebel spirit has slowly taken over, it's harder for me to discern.

Jezebel spirits love to call themselves "true intercessors," "prophets," "prophetesses," and so forth. I believe in and respect intercessors and prophets. But nobody with a Jezebel spirit is going to control this church or the people of the church I oversee.

Jezebel On The Board Of Deacons

We had a Jezebel spirit that developed over time on our official church board. A deacon began to develop more and more the spirit of Jezebel. You can usually identify when a person is coming under the influence of Jezebel because they begin to be careless in their words about those in authority. Jezebel hates any kind of authority. We heard this person saying negative, downgrading things about the president and saying things about congressmen and senators. The next thing we knew, he started saying derogatory things about preachers who are on television and radio. Soon there was a noticeable, attitudinal change in this guy's life. After a short while, his attitude against authority became blatant.

I took a three-month paid sabbatical, the only one in over twenty years. Instead of letting people know that it was a paid sabbatical, he went around telling everybody that the pastor stole ten thousand dollars from the church. It was true that I took three months off, and the church board gave ten thousand dollars for expenses, tuition, books, and training for my three months off. It was not true, however, that I stole ten thousand dollars from the church.

Our senior elder wisely called him in, along with all the people he had infected, sat them around the table in the boardroom, and said, "I suspect that this man has come to each one of you individually telling you that you're the only one he can trust." At that point they all started looking at each other. They were shocked to discover that the man went to each of them and said basically the same thing, "You're the only one

I can trust. I'm only telling you this because I can trust you."

Well, as a result, of course, that man left the church with his Jezebel spirit, and the people that he infected with his poison, half truths, and deception left also. Thankfully, we were able to help some of his victims survive.

So this Jezebel spirit flatters you by making you think, "You're the only one I can talk to about this. You're the only person I can really trust in this whole church."

Whenever you hear someone say this to you, chances are there are at least ten or fifteen others they've gone to and said the same thing. That's the way Jezebel operates; that's the way the Jezebel spirit functions. It thrives on building pride in people, but that pride soon leads to the spirit of fear.

Who Jezebel Targets

Jezebel targets those who are in rebellion, those who are weak, those who are wounded, those who are facing a conflict or are under discipline by true spiritual authority. Jezebel can't stand it when any of her "eunuchs" get in touch with true spiritual authority, people who can speak true words from the Holy Spirit into their lives.

For example, if you're under the control of a Jezebel spirit and you attend a particular conference, that

Jezebel spirit will be right there finding out what was said at that conference. She will drill you with questions about what you heard. The Jezebel spirit will interject little subtleties and questioning remarks after the pastor's sermon or after you've been in contact with any true spiritual authority so that anything the Holy Spirit has spoken into your life will be diluted.

Jezebel seduces by using witchcraft.

Chapter 9

How Jezebel Manipulates

Now, let me talk to you about how Jezebel spirits use manipulation and intimidation to control and dominate. This is going to be the most helpful part to you.

Essentially the Jezebel spirit says, "I don't care who's in authority as long as I have control." "I don't care who the pastor is as long as I'm the person influencing him." "I don't care if this man is my husband as long as I can control him." "I'm not interested in who the leader is as long as I can control him."

The Jezebel spirit is a spirit of control. Jezebel resorts to all kinds of manipulation and human maneuvering to get her way, even if her way isn't right. You simply cannot please a person with a Jezebel spirit no matter how sensitive you try to be with her feelings. Anything you do will come back in a twisted form.

How Jezebel Manipulates People

In a nutshell, here's how people with a spirit of Jezebel manipulate. I'm going to give you eight possible ways this spirit of control may try to manipulate your life.

■ *Number One: false tears.*

They pretend to be hurt, and of course, you're the one that caused the hurt. They believe the tears will move you to act according to the way they think you should act. Just like little children, they cry and cry until they get their way because they've discovered they can manipulate with false tears.

■ *Number Two: outbursts with intermittent kindness.*

This is a Korean brain washing technique used during the Korean War. Captors would be extremely cruel to the prisoners, and then the next day they'd be extremely kind to the prisoners. The next day they'd once again be extraordinarily cruel to the prisoners and the next day really nice. The prisoners got to the point where they didn't want to do anything that would anger their captors because they didn't want to face another outburst. Soon they came under complete submission to their enemy.

■ *Number Three: guilt.*

The Jezebel spirit keeps tabs on favors so she can use them in the future. This is what Absolam did.

Absolam, who betrayed his father David, went out to the city gate and waited for people with emotional hurts and wounds to come along. He started giving them favors and pretending that he was feeling sorry for them. When Absolam needed something he'd say, "You owe me."

If Jezebel wants you to do something unethical or illegal or against your values and principles, you'll hear something like this: "After all I've done for you, you won't do this simple thing for me?" Suppose she wants you to misrepresent the truth and you won't do it. Here it comes in one form or another, "After all I've done for you."

When we expelled a Jezebelian pastor from one of our branch churches, he whined, "After sixteen years of love and service I've given that church, this is how I'm repaid." Well, yes, if you want to flow in a false spirit instead of the Holy Spirit, you'd better believe we're going to take you out of leadership. And we're not going to feel guilty about it.

■ *Number Four: money.*

In some cases Jezebel provides a lot of money to the church, but her motive is not to bless the church but to control the church. I recently dealt with a situation where a man with a Jezebel spirit, sitting on the board of a church, had driven off every pastor that church ever had. That man sat on that church board so arrogantly and proudly. He would buy cars for the bishop's son so that he'd win the bishop's favor. And he did. The carnal bishop supported the Jezebelian board member every time there was a conflict.

Finally, the church rose up and decided they didn't want this man in their church controlling, manipulating, and driving off pastors whenever a pastor confronted him. "OK, I'll just take my money and withhold it from the offering." Invariably, the church couldn't make their payments, so they had to get rid of the pastor instead of the man with the spirit of Jezebel.

■ *Number Five: sympathy solicitation.*

"Poor old me, I got a raw deal. You just don't know what's happened to me. You can't believe what *they've* done to me after all I've done for them." The problem is Jezebel is usually very vague in her charges. She can't usually tell you honestly anything specific that was done. She doesn't care about facts or truth. She wants only to influence.

■ *Number Six: selective information.*

This is another way she hopes to control.

Jezebel spirits tell you only a part or a portion of the matter they want you to know. You may feel like something is amiss, but you don't know what. So you believe the person, thinking, "After all, I know this person." Well, that's why John said, "Test the spirits" (I John 4:1).

A fellow with a Jezebel spirit used to tell me things like this: "You know, Pastor, a lot of people are really upset about the decision you made."

I would then demand, "Give me the names of those people."

"Oh no, I wouldn't feel comfortable giving you their names," he'd moan.

If somebody tells me that a lot of people are upset with me, then they're going to give me the names of those people.

Watch out when people come to you and say, "This is what I heard. I'm not supposed to tell you where I heard it." That's when you need to say, "Then don't tell it. If you can't give me names of where you heard it, and verify who said it, then just shut up and don't talk to me about it."

■ *Number Seven: threats.*

This is a trademark of Jezebel. She threatened Elijah, she threatened John the Baptist, and she's going to threaten the Greater Works Generation. But you can stand up to her threats and say, "NO!" The one word Jezebel hates is "NO!"

Jezebel is big on threats. You can read her account in I Kings 19:2. Her style is, "If you don't do this, then I'm afraid I'm going to be forced to do that."

"I'm afraid I'm going to have to leave and go to another church if you don't change and do what I say is right."

I tell you, we're *not* raising up an army of people controlled by the devil, governed by the flesh, and a bunch of spiritual pip-squeaks. We're raising up an army — a Greater Works Generation that's going to take the devil's territory and bring thousands into the Kingdom of God. I don't have time for Jezebel's sick games.

■ *Number Eight: counterfeit revelation.*

Jesus said, "She calleth herself a prophetess." She is self-appointed and flows in counterfeit revelation. Jezebel is a counterfeit prophetess, a counterfeit intercessor, a counterfeit deacon, and often a counterfeit Christian. A counterfeit is any "intercessor" or any "prophet" who says they've heard from God about another person and then tell others about what they heard.

When you hear something like this, "God showed me something about the pastor in a dream last night that you need to know so you can pray that he'll properly repent," you've just run into the Jezebel spirit. That is not the Spirit of God.

When Nathan received a word from the Lord about David, he told nobody. Instead he went right to David. Anybody that goes to somebody else and says, "Bill, I got this word about Frank, but don't tell Frank." All you have to do is say, "NO! I won't listen to you. You are subjecting yourself to a miserable Jezebel spirit. I mark you. You are not an intercessor, you are not a prophetess, and you are under the control of Satan." That will put Jezebel in her place and maybe even spark her victim to repentance.

Jezebel must control; there's a need for power, a need for control. It may even be through certain looks on the face but be assured that Jezebel craves control. Do not tolerate Jezebel, even for one minute when you recognize it. Once you deal with it, a whole pile of things will begin to surface that will tell you that you were right. It was indeed the spirit of Jezebel.

Recently, we lost a Michigan church by trying to negotiate with a man that had the Jezebel spirit. You can't negotiate, and you cannot please the Jezebel spirit. There is an antidote though. Pray daily for the gift of discerning of spirits. This is one of the most important gifts a leader can employ.

The antidote for the Jezebel spirit is to stand up to it, and, remember, you're dealing with a spirit and not a person. Every once in awhile all of us get in the flesh and we'd like to control somebody. Stand up firmly against Jezebel. Jezebel despises true authority, and you possess true authority in Jesus Christ.

Authentic authority liberates, it does not dominate. True authority motivates by love, not by fear. True authority protects, does not manipulate and intimidate.

Pastors must be willing to "lay down their lives" to protect the flock from Jezebel spirits.

Chapter 10

How Jezebel Destroyed A Church

Pastor Peckham was leading one of the nation's fastest growing churches. The ministry was prospering, both in numbers and in finances. Other pastors looked to Pastor Peckham for godly guidance and mentoring. The pastor was a featured speaker at almost every major church growth conference in America. He was a hero in his denomination. It looked like nothing could stop this premier ministry.

How Jezebel Destroyed A Once Great Church

On a hot August Sunday, a new group of people began attending the church. Pastor Peckham was thrilled to see so many new people coming week after week. Josie, a saintly-looking woman, seemed to be the leader of this new group now attending. She never missed an opportunity to compliment the pastor on his sermons and immediately became involved in intercessory prayer groups around the church.

Josie and a few of her friends would regularly come to the prayer center and spend hours in prayer. Every so often she would have a good "word from the Lord" for Pastor Peckham. She gained his confidence over time. When there was a problem in the church, she seemed to always have the right word of encouragement for the pastor.

Josie read books about intercessory prayer and prophecy. She announced to the pastor that she believed she was a prophetess. Pastor Peckham had become intrigued with the prophetic movement and was happy to learn that a prophetess was now a part of his inner core. He had a strange "feeling" about Josie but assumed it was only the devil trying to prevent him from having his own personal prophetess who could speak into his life. He didn't recognize the real spirit behind Josie's positioning.

"Pastor," Josie assertively blurted out, "the Holy Spirit is saying to me that He wants to take our church to a new level of worship. God clearly showed me that we need to add some time to the worship portion of the service until God comes down in His glory."

"Well, I certainly want more of God," Pastor replied. "Let's do it."

On Sunday he instructed the worship leader to extend the singing time. It was great the first week.

It is certainly a good thing to worship the Lord, but after time, the singing and standing increased to the point where Pastor's messages from God's Word deteriorated to simple five or ten minute homilies.

Prophecies came forth during the extended times of worship. Josie's group would pray in tongues loudly. It was exciting for Pastor Peckham to see what he thought was the Spirit of God moving in his services in a fresh way. Some people started barking like dogs. When the ushers tried to deal with the disorder, Josie gave a "prophetic word."

"Thus saith the Lord: Hinder not My Spirit, saith God. Quench not My Spirit. This activity is from Me, saith God, and thou shalt not quench My Spirit, for I am bringing to you many miracles you will miss if you quench My Spirit. Allow My people to worship Me, saith God, or I shall bring swift judgement upon thee."

After the so-called prophetic word, some people in the church clapped their hands, happy that God had spoken. Others, more discerning, felt an eerie hollowness in Josie's words.

After a few months, some of the elders noticed that fewer and fewer people were coming to Christ and less and less Bible teaching and preaching was taking place. The church seemed to become weirder and weirder by the day. Josie was meeting with the pastor a couple times a week now, telling him what she saw "in the Spirit" and what he must do to succeed in this fresh "move of God."

Elders talked to Pastor Peckham about all this.

"Pastor, we love and respect you. Yet, we feel that something is amiss. Our church was growing, people were being saved, and people were excited about becoming better disciples for Jesus. But now, many of the older people are leaving the church because they can't stand up for a full 45 minutes every Sunday during the song and worship portion of the service, and our attendance is going down. Pastor, shouldn't we stick to the things that made our church great in the first place?"

"I am concerned too," said the pastor. "I'll pray about it."

At that point, the pastor called Josie to see what the Lord was saying. She assured him that this was just a spiritual transition and that Satan was trying to stir up trouble. She then told him that the Lord showed her that some of the elders were in sin and working for the devil. She sounded very spiritual and in tune with God. She told him that within six months the church would be overflowing with people. Pastor Peckham took courage in her words.

Josie was enjoying having the pastor's ear and, in fact, controlling the decisions made in the church by her "prophetic words."

Shaking continued in the church. More prophecies, wild, disorderly conduct persisted, and the preaching of God's Word all but vanished from the services. People continued to leave the church. Soon, the finances became so weak they couldn't pay their bills. As if that wasn't bad enough, a Sunday School teacher went down the road and started a new church taking half the congregation with him.

Six months came and went. The church was now essentially destroyed, just a shadow of what it was a year earlier. The pastor was humiliated, no longer in demand at the conferences.

Josie, a woman with the spirit of Jezebel, slipped into the church secretly and destroyed it. Pastor Peckham only wanted God's plan for the church, but he lacked good discernment. He thought Josie was a blessing, and she seemed to be at first, but in the end he realized that *she* was the one working for the devil.

She had a Jezebel spirit.

As an official in my own denomination, I see this story repeated time and time again. Jezebel is a deranged spirit, obsessed with control, and she doesn't care how she controls as long as she does. It may be by getting onto a board or committee, or it may be through so-called "words from the Lord," but she will influence, manipulate, and control, or she will leave and take others with her.

Jezebel will not stay in a church where there is a pastor who knows his true spiritual authority and is willing to lay down his life, and his reputation, to protect the flock of God in dealing with the Jezebel spirit. Every sincere Christian wants to be a part of a church where he or she feels protected. I don't want to be a part of a church where a pastor is going to be intimidated or controlled by a Jezebel. Stand up to Jezebel!

Chapter 11

Jezebel's Bitter End

You will never see humility in the Jezebel spirit unless it is false humility designed to manipulate or to make a hypocritical show. Jezebel loves to be in control, but you probably won't see Jezebel on her knees at the altar unless it's to create an impression for the sake of influencing someone. Jezebel hates humility and hates repentance.

Repentance And A Submitted Heart

True repentance will drive the spirit of Jezebel out.

A truly submitted heart to Jesus Christ will repel Jezebel spirits. A believer with a submitted heart says, "I'm not going to depend upon the arm of flesh or worry about what someone else thinks. I'm going to trust God with my life and ministry."

Let God Control

It's so good to just let God control things in our lives; it's liberating. I don't even want a fingernail-sized amount of Jezebel in my life. I want God to be in charge.

How Pastors Can Become Jezebels

The Jezebel spirit doesn't only affect lay people who are obsessed with control. Sometimes a pastor will allow Jezebel to cling to his life and ministry.

It's terrible to be under a pastor who wants to control your life instead of allowing God to do His gentle work in you. Pastors who submit to Jezebel actually try to usurp the Holy Spirit's role.

Take Pastor Wolcott, for example. How excited he was to be selected to start a new church in a capital city. Sincere and godly, Pastor Wolcott studied everything he could find on new church development. He was a marketing master, and his new church grew quickly. He bought a video camera and put himself on cable television and impressed his viewers with what appeared to be a genuine concern for people and authentic miracles happening in his church.

His church grew for five or six years, then a change came over Pastor Wolcott. He started criticizing other ministries in his city. He warned his flock that these other churches would take them down spiritually because "they don't have the deep revelation we do." He started using psychological manipulation on his congregation, much the same way a cult leader does.

It wasn't long before Pastor Wolcott was prophesying over his people. Nobody could take a vacation without his permission. Nobody could get a new job without consulting with him first. He wanted to control nearly every aspect of the parishioners lives. Many turned into emotional cripples, not being able to make simple decisions for themselves. They became dependent upon the pastor's guidance and instructions.

It was difficult to break from his grip. If he found out that a member attended an event at another church, he would emotionally punish them and sometimes preach directly at them making them feel ashamed.

After time, people began to leave Wolcott's church. Many went to other churches for counseling. They were surprised to learn that other churches, too, had good ministries, anointed of the Holy Spirit.

Today Pastor Wolcott's church is more like a small cult. Jezebel has struck again. The pastor became obsessed with control. Instead of allowing the Holy Spirit to do His loving, gentle work on the people, Pastor Wolcott took charge. Once he had a terrific church and was an honored pastor. Today he has no honor or respect in his community.

Jezebel's Bitter End

Now the end of Jezebel is found in II Kings, chapter nine, and it's not pleasant. When Jezebel heard that

Jehu had come to Jezreel, she painted her eyelids and fixed her hair and sat at a window. When Jehu, a man chosen and anointed by Elisha, the prophet, to be the new king, entered the gates of the palace, she shouted at him, "How are you today, you murderer, you son of Zimri who murdered his master?"

He looked up at the window and shouted, "Who is on my side?"

Jezebel's Wimps Finally Say 'Enough Is Enough!'

Two or three of Jezebel's eunuchs (the wimpy men she controlled) looked out at him. These eunuchs were the weak, controlled men she had surrounded herself with and used for years.

When Jehu asked, "Who is on my side?" they decided they had taken enough of Jezebel's manipulation, intimidation, and control.

"If you are on my side, throw her down," Jehu shouted. So, these people, tired of being controlled by the spirit of Jezebel, threw her out the window. Her blood splattered against the wall and on the horses. She was then crushed to death, trampled under horse's hooves.

Jehu then went into the palace for lunch. Afterwards, he told someone to go bury that cursed woman. While he was having lunch, according to the prophecy, the dogs were out there in the street having lunch too. They were eating Jezebel! She had become dog food!

> When Jezebel heard that Jehu had come to Jezreel, she painted her eyelids and fixed her hair and sat at a window.
>
> When Jehu entered the gate of the palace, she shouted at him, "How are you today, you murderer! You son of a Zimri who murdered his master!"
>
> He looked up and saw her at the window and shouted, "Who is on my side?" And two or three eunuchs looked out at him.
>
> "Throw her down!" he yelled. So they threw her out the window, and her blood spattered against the wall and on the horses; and she was trampled by the horses' hoofs.
>
> Then Jehu went into the palace for lunch. Afterwards he said, "Someone go and bury this cursed woman, for she is the daughter of a king."
>
> But when they went out to bury her, they found only her skull, her feet, and her hands.
>
> When they returned and told him, he remarked, "That is just what the Lord said would happen. He told Elijah the prophet that dogs would eat her flesh and that her body would be scattered like manure upon the field, so that no one could tell whose it was."
>
> —2 Kings 9:30-37 (TLB)

You Are Going To A Palace

Here's what's going to happen when you defeat Jezebel. You're like Jehu. You're going to take over a palace. Just as Jehu took over the palace, you're going to come into something big you didn't realize you had available to you. When you learn to *let* God be in control, you are coming into an inheritance. You are going to get a taste of your true royalty in Jesus Christ.

Here's what else is going to happen according to Revelation, chapter two. There is an amazing promise to overcomers. "Him that overcometh and keepeth My works unto the end, to him I will give power over the nations." I like the way the Living Bible puts it. "You will rule them with a rod of iron, just as My Father gave Me authority to rule them; they will be shattered like potted clay that is broken into tiny pieces and I will give you the morning star."

> "To everyone who overcomes—who to the very end keeps on doing things that please me—I will give power over the nations.
>
> You will rule them with a rod of iron just as my Father gave me the authority to rule them; they will be shattered like a pot of clay that is broken into tiny pieces.
>
> —Revelation 2:26-27 (TLB)

In other words, Jesus is saying, "I'm going to give you true authority." And when Satan starts setting up his little strongholds, you're going to shatter them to bits because you've got *true* spiritual authority, no more phony Jezebelian counterfeit. And to possess true spiritual authority you have to be under God's delegated authority. Those who follow Jezebel aren't under any real authority.

I have a Scripture I'm going to share with you in regard to defeating Jezebel. I told you about humility, repentance, and saying "no" to Jezebel. I know it's hard to say "no" to Jezebel when you've been under her control for so long. It may be tough, but it's time to break loose from that spirit. It's time to get your true spiritual authority from Jesus Christ, God's Son. And it's time to go forth and become a part of the "Greater Works Generation."

Shout Triumph Over Jezebel

Shout triumph over your enemy (Psalm 108:9). The Jezebel spirit is your enemy. You are going to shout triumph over the spirit of Jezebel. You want the power of the Holy Spirit not counterfeit power.

Human Help Is Useless

Understand this also: Psalm 108:12-13 tells us that *human help is useless.*

> Give us aid against the enemy, for the help of man is worthless. With God we will gain the victory, and he will trample down our enemies.
>
> —Psalm 108:12-13 (NIV)

There comes a point when every one of us has to stand up to a Jezebel, whether it's a spirit coming to us or a spirit operating through another person. There comes a point when you have to say "no" because no human help is going to give you success. When you turn matters over to the Lord, whatever they may be, He says, "Don't worry, son (or daughter), I'll go to work on it, and I'll take care of it." Then you'll have perfect peace.

There are two keys you can use right now at this very moment.

• Shout a shout of triumph over your enemy. Go ahead. Do it right now.

• Put your trust in the Lord, not human instrumentation.

Psalm 108:12-13 (TLB) says mighty things are going to happen after the foe is trampled. Jehu came with true spiritual authority. Those controlled by Jezebel recognized that true spiritual authority and decided they were tired of false authority, so they threw her out, and the dogs had her for lunch that day.

That was the end of the original Jezebel.

Why You MUST Disassociate From Jezebel Now!

Not only will a bitter and tragic end come to those who operate in the Jezebel spirit, but a horrible curse will come upon their children and all who associate closely with this spirit.

Shortly after Jezebel met her horrible fate, another surprise awaited her children and her grandchildren. All of them were murdered and decapitated. Their heads were put in baskets and sent to the city of Jezreel

(II Kings 10:6-8), the place where Jezebel had ordered the murder of Naboth, the vineyard owner.

Jesus said:

> Behold, I will cast her into a bed, and them that commit adultery with her into great tribulation, except they repent of their deeds.
>
> And I will kill her children with death; and all the churches shall know that I am he which searcheth the reins and hearts: and I will give unto every one of you according to your works.
>
> —Revelation 2:22-23

So you see, not only will the person with the Jezebel spirit be judged, but her family and all those who associate with her as well. Trouble, tribulation, and even death are promised for those who warm up to one with a Jezebel spirit.

I've seen it time and time again. I always wondered why it happened that way, but now I know after doing the research for this book. It's so clear. A person will align with a Jezebel intercessor or prophet, and after awhile their life begins falling apart. They experience trouble and tribulation, usually starting in their home with their children, and eventually *something* or *someone* dies. A ministry dies, a talent dies, a love dies. No wonder, Jezebel ministers death.

Derrick was an anointed associate minister in one of the nation's largest churches. He wanted revival and God's presence desperately, but in his quest, didn't always pursue the right avenues. In his desire to see the supernatural, he did not discern the spirits and began listening regularly to a Jezebelian prophetess. He was impressed with this woman's spirituality but didn't know she was a Jezebel. He brought her into his inner circle of close friends. He had no idea she was dealing in Jezebelian witchcraft.

Derrick became weirder and weirder, listening to this prophetess. He began developing some strange views about God's nature as a result. Derrick's pastor warned him that this woman was not anointed by God. Instead of listening to his pastoral authority, he wanted to hear directly "from God" through this prophetess. "After all," he expressed to those close to him, "the pastor is jealous and just wants to hinder the supernatural in my ministry."

It wasn't long before problems developed in his home, with his wife, then his children. At the worst possible time, while Derrick was practically drowning in debt because of his wife's spending habits, the pastor called him into his office and terminated his ministry at the church. Now Derrick blames the pastor for not being spiritually enlightened. Derrick and his friends think he's a victim of the pastor's insensitivity, but he's really a victim of the Jezebel spirit. The pastor knew the history of that Jezebelian woman who called herself a prophetess. She's destroyed others and done it all with a sweet smile.

Just as the original Jezebel enjoyed killing true prophets of God, the Jezebel spirit today delights in killing good ministries and naive ministers. And just as it happened to all those who closely associated with Jezebel and her evil husband, it will happen to those who closely associate with a Jezebel spirit today. They probably won't be murdered, but something will die in their lives or their ministries.

> Jehu then killed all the rest of the members of the family of Ahab who were in Jezreel, as well as all of his important officials, personal friends, and private chaplains. Finally, no one was left who had been close to him in any way.
>
> —2 Kings 10:11 (TLB)

The Promises For Those Who Break Loose From The Controlling Grip Of Jezebel

Just like Jehu inherited a palace, I believe you are going to inherit some real estate or finally receive a blessing or gift you've only dreamed about in the past. Jezebel has been keeping the blessings of God from reaching you until now. Get ready for something good to happen when you break loose from the torturous grip of the Jezebel spirit.

Jesus promised to give you *power* over nations, along with the Morning Star, when you overcome this spirit. That's right, Jesus Himself will be right next to you giving you an inheritance along with supernatural power. You will walk with Him, personally, no longer controlled through lower, carnal tactics.

> And he that overcometh, and keepeth my works unto the end, to him will I give power over the nations:

> **And he shall rule them with a rod of iron; as the vessels of a potter shall they be broken to shivers: even as I received of my Father.**
>
> **And I will give him the morning star.**
>
> **He that hath an ear, let him hear what the Spirit saith unto the churches.**
>
> **—Revelation 2:26-29**

You can bring an end to the Jezebel in your life. *You don't have to take it anymore!* Now, in the Name of our Lord Jesus, do it! Just as Jehu took over Jezebel's palace you, too, will conquer and enjoy new territories and blessings once you defeat your Jezebel.

Chapter 12

The Sin Of Witchcraft

A Jezebel Employee

I got a letter from a former employee who had all the signs of Jezebel. This woman was upset because we had to confront her about an inappropriate relationship and inordinate gossip. Yet, she always tried to present herself as a powerful praying woman of God.

She refused to show up for work for several weeks because she thought I had referred to her in a sermon on Jezebel. She thought I was talking directly to her. I wasn't, but it turns out that the Jezebelian spirit did very clearly manifest itself in her. It was unbelievable.

She sent me a letter saying that she didn't have a Jezebel spirit, but that the elders, deacons, associate pastors, and I were all Jezebels. She said our elders were perverts, and our pastors were twisted. She made some other unfounded, outrageous accusations about the church and key leaders. She couldn't stand it that she had to be corrected. Jezebel is not teachable in the least.

In the next paragraph, after criticizing our staff and asserting that she was no Jezebel, she wrote:

1. Send my paycheck to my house right away.

2. Send me an official letter of termination.

3. Gather up all my personal belongings, and have them delivered to me.

4. Send me copies of the minutes of your meetings.

5. After you meet my demands, I will return my church key.

Clearly Jezebel. The policy is, when an hourly employee resigns, they must bring their key into the security office. Afterward they can pick up their final paycheck and gather their personal belongings. Jezebel doesn't care about policy. Look at the demands she made contrary to our official policy. "It's going to be my way," Jezebel says. "I'll dictate how it's all going to be done."

Jezebel will be Jezebel right up to the end. She must not be tolerated in a church, a home, a business, or a school. She can't stand it when someone stands up to her schemes and calls them for what they are: witchcraft.

Jezebel relies on witchcraft to do her manipulating. Let's take a closer look at this subject.

> For, brethren, ye have been called unto liberty; only *use* not liberty for an occasion to the flesh, but by love serve one another.
>
> For all the law is fulfilled in one word, *even* in this; Thou shalt love thy neighbour as thyself.
>
> But if ye bite and devour one another, take heed that ye be not consumed one of another.
>
> *This* I say then, Walk in the Spirit, and ye shall not fulfil the lust of the flesh.
>
> For the flesh lusteth against the Spirit, and the Spirit against the flesh: and these are contrary the one to the other: so that ye cannot do the things that ye would.
>
> But if ye be led of the Spirit, ye are not under the law.
>
> Now the works of the flesh are manifest, which are *these*; Adultery, fornication, uncleanness, lasciviousness,
>
> Idolatry, witchcraft, hatred, variance, emulations, wrath, strife, seditions, heresies,
>
> Envyings, murders, drunkenness, revellings, and such like: of the which I tell you before, as I have also told *you* in time past, that they which do such things shall not inherit the kingdom of God.
>
> —Galatians 5:13-21

One word in the list of works of the flesh I want to focus on is witchcraft. Some translations translate it "sorcery." The subject of witchcraft is found in the Old Testament as well as in the New Testament. The sin of witchcraft has its origin in the flesh. The term "flesh" refers to the unregenerate human nature. Fleshly witch-craft can quickly degenerate into deathly demonic power if it is not dealt with.

Infiltrating Churches

A well known evangelist said that a number of con-verted witches are warning church leaders that prac-ticing witches are now infiltrating churches, especially charismatic churches. Some of these former witches have authored books telling of their diabolical plot to enter congregations posing as super-spiritual Chris-tians with the purpose of deceiving and shipwrecking pastors, resulting in multitudes of naive believers be-ing led into false worship.

Many of these witches are already firmly estab-lished in churches, controlling both the pastor and con-gregation, and causing great confusion, wickedness, divorce, and even death. This evangelist went on to say that he knows of a large church wholly given over to Satan. I, too, am familiar with the church of which he speaks.

The pastor had a lustful, evil spirit. He committed one act of adultery after another, and soon his wife became involved. The pastor and his wife eventually introduced something into the congregation called "spiritual connections." They developed an entire doc-trine around this revelation of spiritual connections.

First, they brought ballroom dancing into the sanc-tuary. The pastor told the people to look into their partner's eyes until the Holy Spirit made a connection. Pastors, leaders, and deacons became involved. They began swapping wives, committing adultery. Before long it was chaotic, and divorce became rampant in the church. Parishioners began having nervous breakdowns; the pastor's son committed suicide. His daughter divorced and ran off with another man. More suicides were reported among members. One young mother was so distraught over her husband's leaving, she drowned her baby in the bathtub so that her baby's soul would be safe with Jesus.

Today that church has been utterly destroyed because of a Jezebelian witchcraft practice that slipped into that church.

A Witch In Church

I was preaching in another city a few years back, and I sensed something in my spirit. I know when Satan is at work. I had prayed. I had prayer partners praying. We had some good results in the service, but during the whole meeting, it was very difficult for me. I was having a struggle. I can only describe it like this: A big fan in the back of the auditorium was blowing my words back to me. It was almost like I had to repeat them again and again before they would sink in.

I looked in the back and noticed a lady just sitting there with her head bowed, and the Holy Spirit spoke to me, "There's the problem." There was a witch in the service. So, at the end of the service I went over to the pastor and asked who that lady was sitting over there in the back, all dressed in black. He said, "I've never seen her before in my life." I told him, "You better find out. I believe the Holy Spirit told me she is a witch sent in here to create confusion."

Well, the pastor rounded her up, and, sure enough, she was a member of a coven of witches near the city. They had sent her into the church to cause confusion and create problems, but they forgot about one thing…the Holy Spirit. The lady in black gave her life to Jesus Christ.

When we think of witchcraft, we usually think of ugly women flying on brooms with big warts on their noses. Or we think about the practice of wiccan, covens, black magic, neo-pagans, and black robes, but there's a kind of witchcraft that is more dangerous than the obvious kinds.

There are reports estimating there may actually be as many as 5-10 million practicing witches in the United States today. The Armed Forces Bureau estimates a half million practicing witches in the United States. Whenever you hear the term, "Mother Earth" or "Earth Day," you are hearing terms of witchcraft.

Witchcraft, at least in its lower stages, is a whole lot more subtle than those meeting together in black robes and using pentagrams, inverted crosses, and chants.

If you have ever had words spoken into your life that still haunt you today, it could be that the devil stuck a stinger in you through the practice of witchcraft. Even Christians get involved in witchcraft without even knowing it. How? By utilizing sarcasm, ridicule, threats, accusations, gossip, and slander. We'll look more closely at these in the next chapter.

Whenever there is confusion, discouragement, or depression, there is likely a Jezebelian spirit of witchcraft somewhere.

Chapter 13

Using Words To Harm

In the Hebrew, the Greek, and the Aramaic languages, *a witch is a person who uses spoken words to harm others or uses poison (literal or figurative) to harm or control others.*

The Power Of Control Is Quite Attractive

There are books on the market that teach how to control other people. I received such an advertisement in the mail. It was an ugly advertisement, but it did attract my attention. The title of the book they were selling for $39.95 was *"How to Get Anybody To Do Anything You Want."*

Now that's an attractive concept, and a lot of us would like to get certain people to do what we want. There is a part of the unregenerate nature that wants to control other people.

Many teenagers today are being attracted to witch-craft because they believe it will enable them to gain control over the lives of other people. They want to be able to manipulate circumstances for their own favor.

Toxic Words

A witch is a poisoner, one who uses toxic potions or toxic words in order to hurt, control, or kill humans by stealth. When I say "stealth," I think you get the picture. You are unaware of the stealth bomber. Radar can't pick it up, and so when a person is out to destroy you by stealth, it means you think they're your friend. They don't pop up on your radar screen as an enemy fighter. They're in stealth, in disguise.

Jesus referred to "wolves in sheep's clothing." Sarcasm, threats, and statements that induce guilt are forms of the early stages of witchcraft. Jezebel employed these methods, and the spirit of Jezebel does the same today.

> Beware of false prophets, which come to you in sheep's clothing, but inwardly they are ravening wolves.
>
> —Matthew 7:15

Words Can Be Like Stingers

Paul talked about witchcraft as being one of the works of the flesh. I usually forget offenses quickly, but there are certain times that people have said things that have been like stingers.

For example, I was on vacation with my family one year. We didn't take a lot of vacations, but this particular year we rented a little cabin up on Chippewa Lake. We had no telephone, and I'm not even sure we had running water in that little cabin. When I got home after a week off, I found out that a fellow in the church had died. He was the kind who would show up at church once in a while, and his wife always tried to act like she was superior to everyone else and extraordinarily holy in her own right.

As soon as I got home and found out this fellow had died, I called to tell the family how sorry I was. The wife said to me, "Yes, we needed you, but you weren't here for us. You were out having fun when we needed you the most."

I learned long ago that I am not the Holy Spirit. I can only be in one place at a time. Yet after she spoke those words, I started feeling guilty about something for which I shouldn't have been feeling guilty. I felt discouraged over that simple statement of hers. I listened as she glorified her husband like he was some fabulous Christian prophet of some sort. (I thought the guy was a flake, to tell you the truth.)

She was dealing in witchcraft, and she didn't know it. Whenever someone tries to subtly plant a guilt trip on you, they are operating in fleshly witchcraft. Intimidation is nothing but a form of fleshly witchcraft. The problem is when people start using fleshly witchcraft they attract demons that can take them into the demonic levels of witchcraft.

The Scriptures tell us about Jezebel's witchcrafts (plural). This tells us that she operated in both fleshly witchcraft as well as demonic witchcraft.

I've found that people dealing in witchcraft are attracted to certain kinds of ministry in a church. One, for example, is intercession. Another is the prophetic ministry.

In the ministry of intercession you're talking *to God* on behalf of people, and in the prophetic ministry you're talking *to people* on behalf of God. Both are authoritative ministries.

Don't misunderstand me. Intercessory ministry is one of the highest callings in life, and I want intercessors around me all the time. I have people praying for me constantly, but there are certain "Jezebels" that the only reason they want to be part of an intercessory group is so they can know what's going on. Jezebel needs inside information that she can twist and pervert.

There are some who flow in a so-called prophetic ministry so they can control and dominate a church. I've heard many false prophecies in my lifetime. Again, don't misunderstand me. I love words of prophecy. They're beautiful *when they are genuine.*

But some people give "prophetic words" in order to strike fear or dread in believers' hearts for the purpose of controlling. This is witchcraft.

The sending of unsigned notes of "correction" is a form of witchcraft. I used to get unsigned notes that would have Scriptures taken out of context, and there would be no signature. I used to read them, and it was like a stinger in my mind. I would want to respond to somebody, but I didn't know who to respond to. Why did these unsigned "sniper" notes bother me so badly? It's because witchcraft was behind every one of them.

Unsigned "Sniper" Notes

One day while I was praying, God said to my heart, "Don't read any unsigned letters. They're from the devil." Every one of them were forms of witchcraft and poison, designed to harm, control, or manipulate. *Witchcraft in its simplest form begins as a work of the flesh designed to manipulate or control you.*

Jezebel was full of witchcrafts (plural). She operated in different levels of witchcraft, both fleshly witchcraft and demonic witchcraft. That's why, when she spoke forth her threats and sarcasm, her words were so powerfully discouraging to men of God. They were like spiritual bee stingers.

Stingers of witchcraft are designed to get your mind off God and onto a problem or situation.

The Bible says in II Kings 9:22 that she was full of witchcrafts. She was obsessed with controlling people and situations.

How Witchcraft Works

Here's how witchcraft works. You get this problem or situation presented to you. It may come through intimidation, guilt, fear, or any kind of words spoken that make you feel hollow and empty in the pit of your stomach.

You try to pray, but your mind keeps going back to the words that were spoken or the problem you're trying to figure out. Just when you think you've got it figured out, it seems to degenerate into a fresh twist.

Elijah just slew 850 prophets, 400 of one kind and 450 of another kind, a great victory, and was trusting God for revival in Israel. Jezebel, that wicked woman practicing witchcraft, sent out a threat on Elijah's life, and he ran away. He went running for his life. He became discouraged and depressed.

Words are powerful, and this woman spoke words of witchcraft that were so incredibly potent, they discouraged the mighty prophet. Now he wants to die.

The Father Of Lies

Have you ever been threatened by somebody? Have you ever been made to feel guilty for something you didn't do or couldn't prevent? Has someone ever said that you said or promised something that you know you didn't? It really bothers you. Do you know why? It's because the father of lies is at work; it's the spirit of witchcraft working through somebody who wants to hurt or control you.

A witch is a person who goes around spreading dissension, poisoning people's minds.

I heard about this guy and his wife going into a pet store. A parrot says, "Hey buddy, your wife sure is ugly, and she smells bad too. She doesn't even know how to dress!" The wife started crying, so the husband told the store manager that the parrot just offended his wife and ruined her day. So, the store manager went over and smacked the parrot. As the man and his wife were on their way out, the parrot chirped, "Hey buddy." The guy looked at him, and the parrot said, "You know!"

They were only words of a parrot, but they ruined that woman's day. Has there ever been something that someone said to you that ruined your day? You see, we can't control what other people say to us, but we can control our response to it.

It's Always Your Fault, Never Jezebel's

People operating in witchcraft always seem to twist things around. The spirit behind them is perverse and deranged.

When somebody with a Jezebel spirit betrays you, he will always turn the tables around and make you feel like you're the betrayer.

When a "Jezebel" criticizes you, she will always turn it around trying to make it look like something is wrong with you, not her.

Well, I've got news for you, beloved. There is nothing wrong with you. You have nothing to be ashamed of; you've got nothing to feel guilty about.

If what is said has no truth in it, the shield of faith will quench it before it ever becomes a stinger in you. If you let it become a stinger in you, it will grow into a root of bitterness, and then you will pick up that spirit of witchcraft and try to control the situation. You'll try to control the other person instead of doing what Jesus said to do by praying for those that despitefully use you. Turn it over to God, and say, "God, will you handle this? This is a mess."

Whenever there is confusion, discouragement or depression, there is likely a Jezebelian spirit of witchcraft somewhere.

Gossip and undercover secret prayer meetings are probably controlled by a spirit of witchcraft.

In Ezekiel 13:17-23 we're told there were Hebrew prophetesses practicing witchcraft, magical arts for the preservation of some and for the destruction of others.

"Son of dust, speak out against the women prophets too who pretend the Lord has given them his messages.

Tell them, 'The Lord God says: Woe to these women who are damning the souls of my people, of both young and old alike, by tying magic charms on their wrists, furnishing them with magic veils, and selling them indulgences. They refuse to even offer help unless they get a profit from it.

For the sake of a few paltry handfuls of barley or a piece of bread will you turn away my people from me? You have led those to death who should not die! And you have promised life to those who should not live by lying to my people—and how they love it!' "

And so the Lord says: "I will crush you because you hunt my people's souls with all your magic charms. I will tear off the charms and set my people free like birds from cages.

I will tear off the magic veils and save my people from you; they will no longer be your victims, and you shall know I am the Lord.

Your lies have discouraged the righteous when I didn't want it so. And you have encouraged the wicked by promising life, though they continue in their sins.

But you will lie no more; no longer will you talk of seeing 'visions' that you never saw nor practice your magic, for I will deliver my people out of your hands by destroying you, and you shall know I am the Lord."

—Ezekiel 13:17-23 (TLB)

I found out in 1985 that some people were having a prayer meeting to ask God to take me out. That's witchcraft, not a prayer meeting. They were having prayer meetings demanding that God would either move me out or kill me.

There are plenty of Jezebelian witchcraft stingers coming your way every week, if not every day. That's why we have the shield of faith, to quench all the fiery stingers of the devil.

Now the contrast to Jezebel is this: Believers and lovers of Jesus Christ walk humbly in a personal experience with the living God. We attempt to live a life in conformity with God's will and to do things that will bring glory to God.

Clara, The Intercessor Witch

Clara started attending the church twelve years ago. She seemed to be a saintly woman and was drawn to the prayer ministries of the church.

She gained Pastor Korman's confidence when he noticed how much she was praying at the church. He even gave her a key to the church so she could come in and pray during off hours. Clara had access to the pastor and became one of his personal intercessors.

Pastor Korman noticed some strange things about Clara but was willing to overlook them because of her constant prayer for him and the church. Whenever something really good happened in the church, Clara told him, "That's exactly what I've been praying about. God showed me that would happen."

After time, Clara was confronted by the elders about some of her strange behavior. She laughed, groaned, and broke out in deep wailing at the worst possible times drawing attention to herself. Clara told the elders it was "the spirit of intercession" upon her. She became bolder and bolder in her rebellion toward church policies and orderliness.

One day, she boldly told the pastor that God showed her that he was to start a citywide prayer meeting with pastors of all denominations and that they were to pray for Israel. The pastor certainly was not opposed to corporate pastoral prayer meetings and was all for praying for Israel and the Middle East. But there was one problem: God had not spoken to Pastor Korman about it.

Clara's insistence became a terrible pressure on the pastor. He had to do it now or God would judge him. Pastor Korman wisely stood up to the Jezebel spirit behind Clara's life and said, "When God speaks to me, I will obey. Until then, I will wait on Him."

Clara was immediately offended that the pastor wouldn't obey her urgent instructions. So she gathered a group around her and told them, "I've been praying for Pastor Korman a lot lately. God showed me why he's become insensitive to the Holy Spirit. It goes back to a sexual sin in his childhood that he's struggled with ever since. He's struggling with sexual sin right now, and it's preventing him from obeying God."

She, of course, did not tell this to Pastor Korman, only to others in the guise of requesting prayer for him. One day, after getting dozens of people to pray for Pastor Korman and his "sexual problem," she mustered the courage to talk to an elder who was leading a particular prayer meeting.

She started by flattering the elder and telling him how spiritually in tune he was and what a great prayer meeting he leads. Then, when she thought she had him under her spell, she blurted out her revelation of the pastor's alleged sexual sin.

The elder immediately said, "Okay, Clara, let's go talk to Pastor Korman about this."

"Oh, no. We can't let him know that we know about it."

"Well, Clara, you are spreading poison about our pastor, and he has a right to defend himself. I've known Pastor Korman for twenty years. He's always been open with me about his faults and struggles. Pastor Korman confides in me and has never shown any evidence of some perverse sexual sin. Now, we are going together to talk to him about your revelation."

"No, I'm not going. God told me to pray not to confront," Clara snipped.

The elder continued, "Clara, if you would share this 'revelation' with me and not with the man you are talking about, it just tells me that you are basically a witch, not an intercessor or prophetess."

"God told me that I'm a powerful intercessor and also a prophetess," Clara firmly and aggressively announced.

"Well then, if you were truly a prophetess, you would do like Nathan did and confront the person, not go around telling others about some imaginary sin."

"God speaks to me all the time," Clara asserted. "I have insight nobody else has, and Pastor Korman disobeyed God when I told him to start a citywide prayer meeting to pray for Israel."

"Clara," the wise elder said seriously and firmly, "I mark you right now as a divisive individual, a person given to sins of the tongue. You are not to be considered an intercessor or prophetess in this church unless I see sincere repentance and a change in your rebellious attitude. Now, Clara, the beginning of repentance and change is by you and me going to Pastor Korman and confronting him about your so-called revelation."

"No, I'm not going to him. God told me not to because he will deny it anyway."

"I would expect him to deny it, Clara, because it's not true. You are a marked false prophetess and will have nothing to do in this church ever again."

Clara, under the influence of the Jezebel spirit, huffed away muttering judgments upon the elder, the pastor, and the church.

The elder stood up to Jezebel, and she backed off. We need more people to protect innocent pastors against these Jezebelian spirits that spread their witchcraft-filled poison to others. Jezebel spirits are like viruses that can't wait to spread themselves to others.

You must stand up to Jezebel. You must tell her how it's going to be, not let her tell you how it's going to be.

Witchcraft deals with lower supernatural beings and attempts to force issues using psychic powers. Jezebel operated in psychic power that released demons against the man of God. The person operating in witchcraft doesn't care about whether the issues are true and doesn't care about whether these issues bring glory to God. The practicing witch only cares about self-interest, self-preservation, and self-promotion. In a nutshell, *witchcraft is counterfeit spiritual authority.*

Chapter 14

Power Over Jezebel's Witchcraft

Who is prone to practice witchcraft?

■ *Number One — People with serious insecurities.*

Some people are insecure about their height, their age, their hair or lack of hair. They haven't learned how to be totally content in a simple, devoted relationship with Jesus Christ.

■ *Number Two — People who are obsessed with controlling others.*

They use satanic tactics, fear, intimidation, manipulation, and words that are intended to control people emotionally. They will even use psychic power to release demon powers. In I Kings 19:1-2, Jezebel did this when she released those words against Elijah and discouraged him.

■ *Number Three — People who lack the courage to be straightforward.*

They resort to manipulation to gain influence. They are not honest or sincere. Plus, any authority or position of influence they gain by manipulation will block our ability to receive a true commission from God.

■ *Number Four — People who seek to maintain a position of authority gained by self-promotion or manipulation.*

They fear only *true* spiritual authority. When someone walking in true spiritual authority realizes these people are using witchcraft, these Jezebels will begin to use their poison on them or anyone who threatens their domain. That's why they're good at accusations.

Annas and Ciaphas were both possessed with Jezebel spirits, I believe. Annas was the high priest the Jews accepted. Ciaphas was the high priest the Romans placed in charge. They were relatives and controlled both religion and the religious people during the time of Jesus' ministry with His first disciples.

Annas and Ciaphas were making a wealthy living from religion, and it appeared that Jesus of Nazareth was about to ruin it for them. Jesus performed miracles, gathered crowds of people, and taught more about relationships than religion. He was the Son of God incarnate!

The profiteering Jezebelian priests were losing control of the people, thus felt threatened. They needed to control the religion and the people in order to continue to profit.

So they plotted, planned, and laid a strategy to get rid of Jesus Christ before He could bankrupt their religious enterprise. They lied about Him, spread rumors, and schemed to get the Roman government to humiliate Jesus through flogging and finally crucifixion. Pilate, the Roman governor, was nothing but a pawn in their malignant plot. Imagine the spirit of Jezebel laying a carefully planned strategy to execute the Son of God.

They succeeded. They had Jesus crucified even though the Roman officials found no guilt in Him. If only they had known that God would raise Him from the dead in three days and that Christianity would become a dominate force in the world within thirty short years. But they didn't. They wanted to protect their controlled territory.

They succeeded but only for a short season. In less than 40 years, the Romans came and commandeered the wealth of Jerusalem, murdered hundreds of thousands of Jews, no doubt including the children and grandchildren of Annas and Ciaphas. They lost it all because they had a craving to control.

Today both Ciaphas and Annas are sitting incarcerated in the regions of the damned to await the dreadful Great White Throne Judgment where they will be assigned to Hell forever. They not only lost that which they wanted to control, they lost their chance at eternal life with the King. They now sit totally *out of control* with no hope for their future. This was a high price for allowing a Jezebel spirit to attach itself to them.

■ *Number Five — People with self-image problems.*

Have you ever noticed how people who lack a healthy self-image are forever trying to exert authority over others? A police officer who is shorter than others and has never accepted his height often will be unreasonable and authoritarian.

Diotrephes, in 3 John verse 9, loved preeminence in the church. He loved to have a prominent place in the church. If he couldn't sit up front, he wasn't happy. If he wasn't being honored, he wasn't happy. St. John said something that seemed to threaten Diotrephes.

> I sent a brief letter to the church about this, but proud Diotrephes, who loves to push himself forward as the leader of the Christians there, does not admit my authority over him and refuses to listen to me. When I come I will tell you some of the things he is doing and what wicked things he is saying about me and what insulting language he is using. He not only refuses to welcome the missionary travelers himself but tells others not to, and when they do he tries to put them out of the church.
>
> —3 John 1:9-10 (TLB)

People in counterfeit spiritual authority usually feel very insecure when they are around those with true spiritual authority. When the Apostle John confronted Diotrephes about his attitude, he became proud, and the Bible says he became a *prater*. Diotrephes quickly turned into a prater when he couldn't have the pre-eminence he craved.

A prater is one who poisons. In other words, he became a witch. He began to deal in witchcraft when the Apostle John pointed out his sin and when he didn't get his own way.

How To Deal With Witchcraft

Here's what to do. It's simple, but powerful.

■ *Number One — Plead the Blood of Jesus.*

I do this every day. It may sound strange to you, but one of the most powerful practices in my life is when I first get up in the morning. I pray, *"Father, I plead the blood of Jesus over my life: spirit, mind, and body.* I plead the blood of Jesus over Mary Jo's life, spirit, mind, and body; over Trina's life, spirit, mind, and body; over David's life, spirit, mind, and body;" then I plead the blood of Jesus over my family, Mary Jo's family, over our membership, our leaders, our students, and anyone else I'm praying for.

All kinds of witchcraft will be unleashed over the earth soon. The Bible says we shall overcome by the blood of the Lamb and the word of our testimony. *The*

*blood of Jesus Christ is powerful enough to protect you
and me from the Jezebelian spirit of witchcraft.* Every
morning I plead the blood of Jesus over my life.

> And they overcame him [the devil] by the blood
> of the Lamb, and by the word of their testimony;
> and they loved not their lives unto the death.
>
> —Revelation 12:11 (brackets added)

■ *Number Two — Use the testimony of God's
Word.*

They overcame by the blood of the Lamb and by
the word of their testimony. What is the word of their
testimony? It is the *spoken* Word of God. That is the
sword of the Spirit (Ephesians 6:17). It is the *spoken*
Word of God.

When Jesus was fighting off the devil, he spoke *only*
the Word of God. You must speak *only* the Word of God,
not the way the situation looks, not what rumor you
heard, not what you feel.

Somebody told me, "I'm tired of hearing rumors."

I answered, "I've got a suggestion for you. Disassociate from rumormongers and you won't have to listen to rumors anymore." Use the testimony of God's
Word. That *is* the sword of the Spirit. In a sense, you
can slice up these spirits of witchcraft. There'll be little
pieces all over the floor, so to speak. And make sure
you put on the whole armor of God.

The shield of faith will prevent the fiery darts (stingers) from penetrating.

■ *Number Three — Put on the whole armor of God.*

> Finally, my brethren, be strong in the Lord, and in the power of his might.
>
> Put on the whole armour of God, that ye may be able to stand against the wiles of the devil.
>
> For we wrestle not against flesh and blood, but against principalities, against powers, against the rulers of the darkness of this world, against spiritual wickedness in high places.
>
> Wherefore take unto you the whole armour of God, that ye *may* be able to withstand in the evil day, and having done all, to stand.
>
> Stand therefore, having your loins girt about with truth, and having on the breastplate of righteousness;
>
> And your feet shod with the preparation of the gospel of peace;
>
> Above all, taking the shield of faith, wherewith ye shall be able to quench all the fiery darts of the wicked.
>
> And take the helmet of salvation, and the sword of the Spirit, which is the word of God:
>
> Praying always with all prayer and supplication in the Spirit, and watching thereunto with all perseverance and supplication for all saints;
>
> —Ephesians 6:10-18

■ *Number Four — Submit to God and to His true delegated spiritual authority.*

1 Samuel 15:23 says that rebellion is as the sin of witchcraft. When we rebel against God's constituted

or delegated authority, we are rebelling against God Himself. That's why God told Samuel not to take it personally when people were speaking against him.

> For rebellion *is as* the sin of witchcraft, and stubbornness *is as* iniquity and idolatry. Because thou hast rejected the word of the LORD, he hath also rejected thee from *being* king.
>
> —1 Samuel 15:23

St. James instructs us to submit ourselves to God. The only way to be completely free of counterfeit authority is when we are submitted to true authority.

> But he giveth more grace. Wherefore he saith, God resisteth the proud, but giveth grace unto the humble.
>
> Submit yourselves therefore to God. Resist the devil, and he will flee from you.
>
> Draw nigh to God, and he will draw nigh to you. Cleanse *your* hands, *ye* sinners; and purify *your* hearts, *ye* double minded.
>
> —James 4:6-8

■ *Number Five — Harshly resist.*

Don't put up with spirits of witchcraft. Don't allow Jezebel spirits in your life. Resist them – harshly resist!

Parents, please let me tell you how important your words are to your children. Whenever we say something in anger, it's going to become a stinger to them. Always discipline in love, in a way that is best for the child, never out of personal anger.

> Be sober, be vigilant; because your adversary the
> devil, as a roaring lion, walkth about, seeking
> whom he may devour.
>
> —1 Peter 5:8

Don't tolerate any fear, and don't put up with any intimidation. Don't put up with any threats. Harshly resist the devil. He is out there to devour you. That means he'll chew your little finger off, then he'll chew your hand off. And then he'll rip your arm off and laugh at you all the way.

I don't think we resist steadfastly enough.

The spirit of witchcraft is subtle. *Witchcraft is not so much potions as it is poisons.* Poisons are released through the mouth and become stingers. I want the Holy Spirit not a spirit of witchcraft. When I hear a prophetic word, I want to hear from the throne of God not from some psychic power.

When you sense the Jezebel spirit at work, trying to manipulate you or control you; when you feel her witchcrafts down in the pit of your belly, remember:

P — U — A — S — H

1. **P**lead the blood of Jesus Christ over your life daily.

2. **U**se the testimony of God's Word.

3. **A**rmor – Remember the armor of God.

4. **S**ubmit to God.

5. **H**arshly resist the devil.

If you have used any form of manipulation or intimidation on others, you must humble yourself and repent now, before it's too late. Get rid of the Jezebel spirit, and be set free by the Son of the living God, Jesus Christ.

In closing, there are three books I'd like for you to read if you would like to study this further:

1. *The Jezebel Spirit* by Francis Frangipane, Arrow Publications, P.O. Box 10102, Cedar Rapids, IA 52410

2. *Epic Battles of the Last Days* by Rick Joyner, Whitaker House, 30 Hunt Valley Circle, New Kensington, PA 15068

3. *Under Cover* by John Bevere, Thomas Nelson Publishing, P.O. Box 141000, Nashville, TN 37214

You may also call our bookstore at 1-800-888-7284 to order your copies of each of these excellent books.

About The Author

Dave Williams is pastor of Mount Hope Church and International Outreach Ministries, with world headquarters in Lansing, Michigan. He has served for over 20 years, leading the church in Lansing from 226 to over 4000 today. Dave sends trained ministers into unreached cities to establish disciple-making churches, and, as a result, today has "branch" churches in the United States, Philippines, and in Africa.

Dave is the founder and president of Mount Hope Bible Training Institute, a fully accredited institute for training ministers and lay people for the work of the ministry. He has authored 45 books including the fifteen-time best seller, *The Start of Something Wonderful* (with over 2,000,000 books sold), and more recently, *The Miracle Results of Fasting*, and *The Road To Radical Riches*.

The Pacesetter's Path telecast is Dave's weekly television program seen over a syndicated network of secular stations, and nationally over the Sky Angel satellite system. Dave has produced over 125 audio cassette programs including the nationally acclaimed *School of Pacesetting Leadership* which is being used as a training program in churches around the United States, and in Bible Schools in South Africa and the Philippines. He is a popular speaker at conferences, seminars, and conventions. His speaking ministry has taken him across America, Africa, Europe, Asia, and other parts of the world.

Along with his wife, Mary Jo, Dave established The Dave and Mary Jo Williams Charitable Mission (Strategic Global Mission), a mission's ministry for providing scholarships to pioneer pastors and grants to inner-city children's ministries.

Dave's articles and reviews have appeared in national magazines such as *Advance, The Pentecostal Evangel, Ministries Today, The Lansing Magazine, The Detroit Free Press* and others. Dave, as a private pilot, flies for fun. He is married, has two grown children, and lives in Delta Township, Michigan.

You may write to Pastor Dave Williams:

P.O. Box 80825

Lansing, MI 48908-0825

Please include your special prayer requests when you write, or you may call the Mount Hope Global Prayer Center anytime: (517) 327-PRAY

DECAPOLIS
PUBLISHING

For a catalog of products, call:

1-517-321-2780 or

1-800-888-7284

or visit us on the web at:

www.mounthopechurch.org

For Your Spiritual Growth

Here's the help you need for your spiritual journey. These books will encourage you, and give you guidance as you seek to draw close to Jesus and learn of Him. Prepare yourself for fantastic growth!

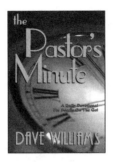

QUESTIONS I HAVE ANSWERED
Get answers to many of the questions you've always wanted to ask a pastor!

THE PASTOR'S MINUTE
A daily devotional for people on the go! Powerful topics will help you grow even when you're in a hurry.

ANGELS: THEY'RE WATCHING YOU!
The Bible tells more than you might think about these powerful beings.

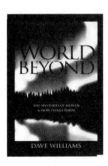

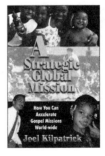

THE WORLD BEYOND
What will Heaven be like? What happens there? Will we see relatives who have gone before us? Who *REALLY* goes to Heaven?

FILLED!
Learn how you can be filled with the mightiest power in the universe. Find out what could be missing from your life.

STRATEGIC GLOBAL MISSION
Read touching stories about God's plan for accelerating the Gospel globally through reaching children and training pastors.

These and other books available from Dave Williams and:

DECAPOLIS PUBLISHING

For Your Spiritual Growth

Here's the help you need for your spiritual journey. These books will encourage you, and give you guidance as you seek to draw close to Jesus and learn of Him. Prepare yourself for fantastic growth!

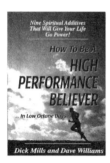

HOW TO BE A HIGH PERFORMANCE BELIEVER
Pour in the nine spiritual additives for real power in your Christian life.

SECRET OF POWER WITH GOD
Tap into the real power with God; the power of prayer. It will change your life!

THE NEW LIFE …
You can get off to a great start on your exciting life with Jesus! Prepare for something wonderful.

MIRACLE RESULTS OF FASTING
You can receive MIRACLE benefits, spiritually and physically, with this practical Christian discipline.

WHAT TO DO IF YOU MISS THE RAPTURE
If you miss the Rapture, there may still be hope, but you need to follow these clear survival tactics.

THE AIDS PLAGUE
Is there hope? Yes, but only Jesus can bring a total and lasting cure to AIDS.

These and other books available from Dave Williams and:

DECAPOLIS PUBLISHING

For Your Spiritual Growth

Here's the help you need for your spiritual journey. These books will encourage you, and give you guidance as you seek to draw close to Jesus and learn of Him. Prepare yourself for fantastic growth!

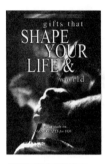

THE ART OF PACESETTING LEADERSHIP
You can become a successful leader with this proven leadership development course.

GIFTS THAT SHAPE YOUR LIFE
Learn which ministry best fits you, and discover your God-given personality gifts, as well as the gifts of others.

GROWING UP IN OUR FATHER'S FAMILY
You can have a family relationship with your heavenly father. Learn how God cares for you.

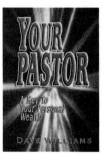

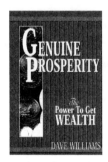

SUPERNATURAL SOULWINNING
How will we reach our family, friends, and neighbors in this short time before Christ's return?

YOUR PASTOR: A KEY TO YOUR PERSONAL WEALTH
By honoring your pastor you can actually be setting yourself up for a financial blessing from God!

GENUINE PROSPERITY
Learn what it means to be truly prosperous! God gives us the power to get wealth!

For Your Spiritual Growth

Here's the help you need for your spiritual journey. These books will encourage you, and give you guidance as you seek to draw close to Jesus and learn of Him. Prepare yourself for fantastic growth!

SOMEBODY OUT THERE NEEDS YOU
Along with the gift of salvation comes the great privilege of spreading the gospel of Jesus Christ.

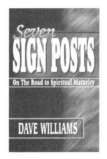

SEVEN SIGNPOSTS TO SPIRITUAL MATURITY
Examine your life to see where you are on the road to spiritual maturity.

THE PASTORS PAY
How much is your pastor worth? Who should set his pay? Discover the scriptural guidelines for paying your pastor.

DECEPTION, DELUSION & DESTRUCTION
Recognize spiritual deception and unmask spiritual blindness.

THE ROAD TO RADICAL RICHES
Are you ready to jump from "barely getting by" to Gods plan for putting you on the road to Radical Riches?

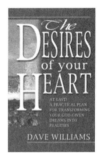

THE DESIRES OF YOUR HEART
Yes, Jesus wants to give you the desires of your heart, and make them realities.

These and other books available from Dave Williams and:

DECAPOLIS PUBLISHING

For Your Successful Life

These video cassettes will give you successful principles to apply to your whole life. Each a different topic, and each a fantastic teaching of how living by God's Word can give you total success!

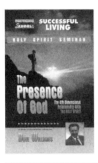

THE PRESENCE OF GOD
Find out how you can have a more dynamic relationship with the Holy Spirit.

FILLED WITH THE HOLY SPIRIT
You can rejoice and share with others in this wonderful experience of God.

GIFTS THAT CHANGE YOUR WORLD
Learn which ministry best fits you, and discover your God-given personality gifts, as well as the gifts of others.

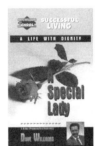

THE SCHOOL OF PACESETTING LEADERSHIP
Leaders are made, not born. You can become a successful leader with this proven leadership development course.

MIRACLE RESULTS OF FASTING
Fasting is your secret weapon in spiritual warfare. Learn how you'll benefit spiritually and physically! Six video messages.

A SPECIAL LADY
If you feel used and abused, this video will show you how you really are in the eyes of Jesus. You are special!

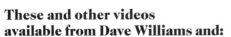

These and other videos available from Dave Williams and:

DECAPOLIS PUBLISHING

For Your Successful Life

These video cassettes will give you successful principles to apply to your whole life. Each a different topic, and each a fantastic teaching of how living by God's Word can give you total success!

HOW TO BE A HIGH PERFORMANCE BELIEVER
Pour in the nine spiritual additives for real power in your Christian life.

THE UGLY WORMS OF JUDGMENT
Recognizing the decay of judgment in your life is your first step back into God's fullness.

WHAT TO DO WHEN YOU FEEL WEAK AND DEFEATED
Learn about God's plan to bring you out of defeat and into His principles of victory!

WHY SOME ARE NOT HEALED
Discover the obstacles that hold people back from receiving their miracle and how God can help them receive the very best!

BREAKING THE POWER OF POVERTY
The principality of mammon will try to keep you in poverty. Put God FIRST and watch Him bring you into a wealthy place.

HERBS FOR HEALTH
A look at the concerns and fears of modern medicine. Learn the correct ways to open the doors to your healing.

These and other videos available from Dave Williams and:

DECAPOLIS PUBLISHING

Running Your Race

These simple but powerful audio cassette singles will help give you the edge you need. Run your race to win!

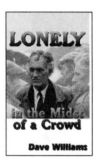

LONELY IN THE MIDST OF A CROWD
Loneliness is a devastating disease. Learn how to trust and count on others to help.

HERBS FOR HEALTH
A look at the concerns and fears of modern medicine. Learn the correct ways to open the doors to your healing.

HOW TO GET ANYTHING YOU WANT
You can learn the way to get anything you want from God!

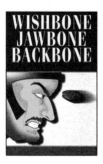

WISHBONE, JAWBONE, BACKBONE
Learn about King David, and how his three "bones" for success can help you in your life quest.

FATAL ENTICEMENTS
Learn how you can avoid the vice-like grip of sin and it's fatal enticements that hold people captive.

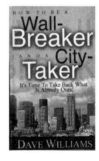

HOW TO BE A WALL BREAKER AND A CITY TAKER
You can be a powerful force for advancing the Kingdom of Jesus Christ!

These and other audio tapes available from Dave Williams and:

 DECAPOLIS PUBLISHING

Expanding Your Faith

These exciting audio teaching series will help you to grow and mature in your walk with Christ. Get ready for amazing new adventures in faith!

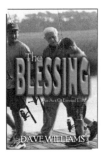

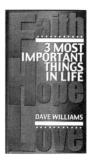

THE BLESSING
Explore the many ways that God can use you to bless others, and how He can correct the missed blessing.

SIN'S GRIP
Learn how you can avoid the vice-like grip of sin and it's fatal enticements that hold people captive.

FAITH, HOPE, & LOVE
Listen and let these three "most important things in life" change you.

**PSALM 91
THE PROMISE OF
PROTECTION**
Everyone is looking for protection in these perilous times. God promises protection for those who rest in Him.

**DEVELOPING
THE SPIRIT OF A
CONQUEROR**
You can be a conqueror through Christ! Also, find out how to *keep* those things that you have conquered.

WHY DO SOME SUFFER
Find out why some people seem to have suffering in their lives, and find out how to avoid it in your life.

These and other audio tapes available from Dave Williams and:

DECAPOLIS PUBLISHING

Expanding Your Faith

These exciting audio teaching series will help you to grow and mature in your walk with Christ. Get ready for amazing new adventures in faith!

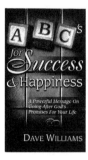

ABCs OF SUCCESS AND HAPPINESS
Learn how to go after God's promises for your life. Happiness and success can be yours today!

FORGIVENESS
The miracle remedy for many of life's problems is found in this basic key for living.

UNTANGLING YOUR TROUBLES
You can be a "trouble untangler" with the help of Jesus!

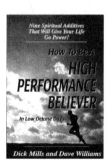

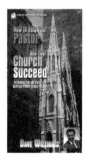

HOW TO BE A HIGH PERFORMANCE BELIEVER
Put in the nine spiritual additives to help run your race and get the prize!

BEING A DISCIPLE AND MAKING DISCIPLES
You can learn to be a "disciple maker" to almost anyone.

HOW TO HELP YOUR PASTOR & CHURCH SUCCEED
You can be an integral part of your church's & pastor's success.

These and other audio tapes available from Dave Williams and:

DECAPOLIS PUBLISHING